Time and Time Again

Pavement Books
London, UK
www.pavementbooks.com

First published 2020 © Don Miller

Cover Image Sue Stanfield
With permission from the artist.

British Library Cataloguing in Publication Data.
A catalogue record for this book is available from the British Library.

ISBN: 978-1-8380137-0-7

Time and Time Again

by
Don Miller

PAVEMENTBOOKS

By the same author

Pervasive Politics: a Study of the Indian District

The Reason of Metaphor

Neighbours and Strangers

Will to Win: The West at Play

In praise of *Time and Time Again*

In his own inimitable, commanding and thoughtful way, Don Miller takes us on a journey through the myriad ways in which time and timing matter. From games of tennis, to cooking, from politics in Australia and the world, through to economic battles, global and local, Miller hones in on the role of time and timing. He turns descriptions of the everyday into a means of demonstrating the paradoxical, fluid and arbitrary quality of that ethereal concept called time. To reflect on time through such everyday reflections situates the bigger questions of life in the heart of the quotidian and no one does this quite like Miller.

Michael Dutton, Professor of Politics, Goldsmiths, University of London

Miller uses words and ideas to make the reader reconsider not only the 'facts' but their own assumptions, including how to think. These essays draw on a wide range of sources, enrolling them in a game that is never predictable; and whose motive forces seems to be curiosity and contingency. He spans domains from sport to art to politics and beyond. The result is fascinating and illuminating; frequently provocative, but never linear and certainly never boring.

Scott McQuire, Professor, Media and Commmunication, Melbourne University of Melbourne

Timing, politics and ethics – those three are dominant in Don Miller's work. Almost playfully, he seduces me as a reader to think through, and through again into what drives us most, and how drivers of current (western) society fool us into thinking that we 'manage' life via the multiple and arrogant attempts to control the times of our lives. Whereas chance, patience and, perhaps laissez-faire, would help us more in living life to the full. Via Nietsche and Freud, Heidegger and Foucault, Don Miller proves to be one of those rare thinkers who walk their talk by weaving the fabric of insight and reflection as a support to re-think current societal doings and shaking the Western fundament of plannability.

Ida Sabelis, Associate Professor of Organization Sciences, VU Amsterdam

Don Miller plays with our notions of time – and even better, timing – as an elegant master of that earliest and most important mode of learning – play time. In illuminating the play of time and timing in tennis, politics, business, love, and more, Miller teases out myriad surprising and salient moral and political facets of the gift of timing – and its absence.

Richard Tanter, Senior Research Associate, Nautilus Institute; Professor of International Relations, University of Melbourne

I dedicate this book to Jan, Madeline, Harriet, Damien and Axl.

Contents

Acknowledgments

I want to thank all those authors who, unwittingly, have helped me to think. And a special thanks to those individuals who throughout my career have congratulated me for what I had written. Their encouragement was important: it permitted me to continue.

Chapter One. Introduction

Sometime in the 1990s, I started to wonder about the contemporary significance of notions of auspiciousness, and inauspiciousness, in India – I had noticed its presence, on occasions, among middle class Indians. This, of course, led me to think about its history in the West.

I was well aware of its importance in ancient Greek culture; and how it was still pervasive during Renaissance times. But such notions got knocked off their pedestal in the West during the so-called Scientific Century of the 1600s. Nevertheless, remnants of the auspicious are still with us, for example, in the pervasive love of gambling; punting on your luck; or your hunch about some imminent outcome. In casual talk we still commonly refer to 'bad luck' or 'good luck'. Such expressions, though, are not references to something *we* have done; rather they refer to what happens *to* us. Luck is the word we use when something outside our control suddenly appears and effects us for good or bad. We are, as it were, innocent by-standers, when, unexpectedly, something external – a storm, a death, a catastrophe, occurs – and that 'coincidence' (the meeting of 'it' with 'us') brings either benefit or harm. A sheer accident can have an enormous impact. If it is a private matter, a few insiders may rejoice or commiserate with you, perhaps for days. We may benefit from it; or, on the other hand it may dramatically change our life, forever.

Which made me think of politicians; in particular, the way political parties are wary of particular times, indeed, tense in the weeks leading to an election. They know that if some mishap occurs during that period, because of its proximity to an election, the public can react in a draconian way; whereas, if we 'give the public' a few months, it will have forgotten all about it. Timing is crucial.

Only then, with that awareness, did I realise what a fascinating and critical thing 'timing' is; not just for politics, but in life generally. Gone was the casual interest in auspiciousness in India; now pressing me for attention was the word 'timing', and the world of timing. This was the first time in my life, I suspect, that I stopped to think about 'time'; the two words, time and timing, are obviously inseparable. Without further thinking I had already called the phenomenon 'political time'. It was only during the writing of that first article that I confronted the inadequacy of the term.

Then, by chance as I was still working on the article that appears now as 'Political Time – a Matter of Timing', I read about a forthcoming conference on 'Time' at the then recently created Institute of Cultural Studies in New Delhi. What timing! I immediately wrote to the director, indicating my intention to attend, and planning to deliver a paper on the subject of 'Time and Timing' – in three to four months time. A perfectly auspicious illustration of the phenomenon?

The conference was full of interest; a rich range of topics from an international gathering of presenters. After delivering my paper, two men approached me and told me of the existence of an International Society for the Study of Time (ISST), which had been created in the 1950s by a J T Fraser, a Hungarian refugee to America; and that ever since there has been a conference every three years on one or other aspect of Time; and that ISST membership is always around three to four hundred people from all conceivable disciplines. One of the men I was speaking to, an American, was the current president; the other a German mathematician, an ex-president. I joined on the spot.

They also mentioned that a new journal, *Time and Society*, had recently appeared, founded and directed by an English academic, Barbara Adam, who was also an ISST member. The next year, my paper, which I titled 'Political Time: The Problem of Timing and Chance,' appeared in the May 1993 issue of that journal. And I met Professor Adam that same year at the first ISST conference I attended, at Cerisy-la-Salle, in Normandy, France.

What follows may be wholly irrelevant to this book, but I must say something about the glorious, fairy-land location of Cerisy-la-Salle. The castle was built between 1613 and 1623. During the revolution it was declared a 'national property'. Joseph Savory bought it in 1819, and it is still in that family's hands. Since 1952 it has been a conference centre 'notable as a crucible of modern thought'. Photographs of every notable current French thinker clutter the walls of one of its public rooms.

I cannot remember what incident in the following years lead me to think about 'anticipation' as another critical aspect of time; 'looking to the future', trying to anticipate what might happen and when, and how. It was fascinating to discover the implications, the overlapping dangers of the term, and the different nuance of the French compared to the English: 'to be prepared,' compared to 'rush in prematurely' invoked different emotional and psychological dispositions. It led me to so many unexpected places. For reasons I cannot recall, I decided to have my next article published locally. 'Anticipating Future Time' was reproduced in the *Australian Book Review's* March 1998 issue under the unexpected label of National Library Australian Essay.

The theme for the 1999 ISST conference was 'Perspectives at the Millennium'. I took the opportunity to prepare a paper entitled 'Quality Time' and it became, in part, a response to a social science friend who chastised me: 'Why bother about the Millennium? It's just the same as any other year.'

That conference was held, again at a charm-

Chapter Two. Quality Time

'Why bother about the millennium? It's just the same as any other year', a sound, levelheaded social scientist recently admonished me, seemingly oblivious to her own unequivocal weighting of dates and years: her children's birthdays, the anniversary of her brother's death, her friend's special annual New Year Eve's party. Does she treat Mondays the same as Sundays?

Time is not even, neutral, uniform, independent of culture. Time is not regular tick-tock time. It varies, comes loaded, heavy or light or tragic or shaking with one or another passion, be that pain or pleasure – each reflecting very human affairs. Beginnings and ends, births and deaths, critical moments of liminality. Big ends, little ends. The shock of the new, the trauma of the old.

Some times come unexpected, when we are not looking, and they stun us, perhaps for ever after. Other times may come around again and again – ghosts continuing to haunt us – and we target them in advance and prepare for them. Sometimes we begin to grieve again secretly as the moment quietly approaches. The anniversary. The anticipation of the return or of the next trial. Lives and entire cultures are composed of this mosaic of *quality times*. We are, in large measure, what we celebrate, publicly or privately, in joy or in anguish.

Such 'archives' (after Jacques Derrida) overlap and vary. We have a choice of which ones to keep alive, which ones to exhume, which ones to bury fast and deep, which ones over which to weep; but they are chosen for us as much as we choose them. What finally determines our 'intensive times'? Who keeps the archive and periodically reorders the file?

Time is not the calendar or the clock, it is the almanac: dated, highlighted, accentuated. But then, is there ever a simple calendar or time chart composed merely of equal entries? Inescapably marked is the end or the beginning of the week, month, year, century, millennium.

All anniversaries vary but with one common quality: they are heady and hearty matters. Moments when feelings and thinking become focused. Overdetermined. Time off from the quotidian preoccupations of life – 'sacred', in a way.

The newspaper headline read: 'The King is dead: Saint Elvis alive and well'.

For hardcore Elvis fans, the quintessential act of remembrance was not a pilgrimage to kitschy Graceland but a trip to Humes Junior High School. The most devoted fans paid $48 to pack the school auditorium to listen to some of Elvis's friends and associates reminisce about the man whose fame is greater than ever, 20 years after his death: Sandy Martindale, who dated Elvis when she was fourteen ... Colonel Bill Taylor, who commanded Elvis in Germany: 'Elvis could read a map better than anyone in the platoon' ... There was a fair number of younger fans, including about 30 Brazilians. Most can barely speak English, but the language barrier has not prevented them from coming to Memphis every steamy August for the past 15 years, to commemorate the anniversary of their idol's death. This week, about 75,000 fans descended on Memphis for the 20th anniversary, and many of them will gather at the Graceland gates tonight, carrying lighted candles as they file past Elvis's grave, as reported in *The Age*:

> We seem to be at that point where you can intelligently talk about the emergence of a quasi-religious movement', Norman Giradot, Professor of Comparative Religions, is reported saying. 'There are parallels in the origins of Christianity, Buddhism, Confuscianism and the Elvis Movement (*The Age*, 16 August 1997).

Professor Giradot's religious analogy had unexpected confirmation from Las Vegas. Next to the entrance doorway into the Las Vegas Hilton is a Perspex case containing the jumpsuit – complete with multi-coloured sequins, big buckle belt, high collar, flared trousers – that Elvis wore during his first Vegas engagement in the hotel, back in January 1972. There is a gap between the side and the front of the case, just enough to slip the tips of the fingers through, but not enough to actually stretch out your hand fully to touch the garment. This is both tantalising and frustrating to the members of the Official Elvis Presley Fan Club of Australia, who have come to see the suit. They have taken their photos and videos, read and reread the inscription at least half a dozen times, and yet they are still no closer to touching a suit the King actually wore. To be so close after coming so far, and yet still not being able to touch it is, to put it mildly, a little frustrating. Then one of the group notices that some of the sequins from the sleeve are missing. So somebody else must have touched it, but how? Frustration turns to irritation. Then one comes up with the idea of slipping a pen through the gap in the perspex glass, hooking it under the sleeve of the Elvis suit, she pulls the sleeve carefully towards her and then through the corner gap, and the small group of the faithful that have gathered are able to stroke the hem. Which they do repeatedly, with a mixture of reverence and excitement that can barely be contained. 'I feel I am getting closer and closer to him,' says one fan. 'It's like he's just upstairs', says another (*The Age*, 16 August 1997).

There is something especially special about transitional moments; something more uncanny than the rite-de-passage as explored by anthropology. Even the stroke of midnight is a loaded moment – Cinderella is not the only character warned to be home 'before the clock' strikes. Frank McCourt tells his story beginning with the fateful birth of his mother, early in the 1900s in Limerick, on New Year's Eve. With the increasingly desperate help of Nurse O'Halloran and, in order of supplication, St. Gerard Majella, patron saint of expectant mothers, St. Ann, patron saint of difficult labor, and St. Jude, patron saint of desperate cases, the infant's head finally appears at the stroke of midnight. After much more pushing the child is fully 'in the world'. As Nurse O'Halloran notes, 'she is a time-straddler, born with the head in the New Year and her arse in the Old or was it her head in the Old Year and her arse in the New. You'll have to write to the Pope, missus, to find out what year this child was born in' (McCourt 1996). And the child was named Angela for the Angelus that rang out the midnight hour.

Certain special moments can become graced, or cursed, as moments of magic, of evil, of the supernatural – to be held in awe, to be feared, to be revered. The moment of a prophet. Not of a free person, but of someone sent to do the work of 'someone' else. To be born within the aura of a quality transitional moment is seen as both auspicious or inauspicious – or bizarrely both: the passing moment of a century, an era, a millennium.

Fiction, once again, captures it well, like the birth of Saleem Sinai, and a thousand other children, and the remarkable fate that awaits them, as told by

Salman Rushdie:

> I was born in the city of Bombay... once upon a
> time. No, that won't do, there's no getting away
> from the date: I was born in Doctor Narlikar's
> Nursing Home on August 15, 1947. And the time?
> The time matters too. Well then: at night. No, it's
> important to be more... On the stroke of midnight,
> as a matter of fact. Clock-hands joined palms in
> respectful greeting as I came. Oh, spell it out, spell it
> out: at the precise instant of India's arrival at Inde-
> pendence, I tumbled forth into the world. - Thanks
> to the occult tyrannies of those blandly saluting
> clocks I had been mysteriously handcuffed to his-
> tory, my destinies indissolubly chained to those of
> my country. For the next three decades there was
> to be no escape. Soothsayers had prophesied me,
> newspapers celebrated my arrival, politicos ratified
> my authenticity. I was left entirely without a word
> in the matter. - I had become heavily embroiled in
> Fate. (Rushdie 1981)

One need not wait for significant historical eventualities. With just a little skill, many times can be wrought
into moments of great import. Auguries plucked
from the air. Political leaders are adept at such operations, which should not be dismissed entirely as mere
rhetoric: They are inherently 'windows of opportunity' – useful to announce new directions, renewals,
fresh commitments, greater endeavors, recharging of
loyalties, pledges, and dedications.

Kim Beazely, leader of the Australian Labor Party, could have been speaking for any political leader when in October 1997, and so within earshot of the millennium, he found a 'sign' of a brave new future in the defection of a significant political figure to his party. On cue he announced, 'It is a symbol of the fact that we are about renewal, about new ideas, about the sorts of ideas this country needs for the new millennium'. (*The Age*, 15 October 1997)

It has often been noted that interminable sightings of 'ends' abound these days – the end of Marx, of Freud, of feminism, of democracy, of the family, of innocence, of the simple life, of the world as we know it – and we could go on. Has sufficient attention been paid, I wonder, to the plethora of new beginnings, of renewals, resurrections, rebirths? It has been suggested that American culture is drenched with such motifs – a constant bombardment of recipes for one renewal or another. And elsewhere?

But all this could perhaps be easily dismissed as false artifact, as little more than dissembling, subjective, human projection onto otherwise unqualified and equal times. The year 2000 is in certain obvious and un-trivial ways no different from the years 1996 or 2019; a Sunday is composed of exactly the same elements as a Wednesday, an anniversary is nothing other than a cultural contrivance at nostalgia – and an occasion thereby open to abuse which otherwise would not accrue to that date, whenever it may be. Witness the annual two thousand and more Protestant marches with fife and drum through the Catholic quarters of Belfast to 'celebrate' the Battle of the Boyne. This is not the inevitable result of a certain calendar date, but the artificial product of particular human determinations.

Think of the endless number of potential anniversaries we do not celebrate. That we pay homage to some while totally neglecting others is the dubious result of public relations rather than of some principle, historical force, or devotion. June 16, for example, is celebrated in many lands as Bloomsday, but what scant attention is paid to King Edward 1 of England, who was born on that day in 1239, or to Stan Laurel, born June 16 in 1890, or to the Battle of Stoke, 1487, the French retreat from the Maginot Line in 1940, Charlie Chaplin's fourth marriage – to Oona O'Neill in 1943 – the hanging of Imre Nagy, in 1958, or the U.S. Senate vote against the withdrawal of American troops from Vietnam in 1971?

Would the world not be a saner and safer place if we forgot anniversaries, ignored so-called special occasions? Would the quality of our lives be impaired?

The argument against *quality times* could go even further. If something is worth celebrating, it is surely inadequate to pay it homage just once a year, or once a week. Remember Bernard Shaw on the questionable Sunday-only observance of religion: if it has value it should determine behaviors at all times, in all circumstances, not merely at ritualised occasions. Something of worth is a timeless not a timely matter. It is understandable when people such as Gandhi, or the entire Islamic tradition, insist that religion and its moral code cannot be kept apart from politics. Quality must be relevant at all times. In more than one way the personal is *always* the political; that is, not simply some recent feminist creed that embarrasses certain males.

Once a quality is set apart and institutionalised into a periodic observance in time and space, the argument might continue, it is transformed into an empty ritual, a hollow symbol. Note the devaluation of Christmas and Easter. And consider special categories, for example, in art: black art, ethnic art, feminist art – these are not signs of privileged respect; they segregate, marginalise, and demean. A ghetto can be a prison, as we know, not a refuge. The practice of *quality time* slides easily into one of corruption, sham, and betrayal.

In certain significant ways this critique of *quality time* reproduces the spirit of the original Protestant (a word I am using more figuratively than historically) condemnation of Catholicism – of its images, icons, rituals, superstitions and trappings of religious devotion. The new form of Protestant Christianity was stripped to essentials, just as English Protestantism stripped churches bare of all their art, color, and dramatic ceremony. A direct communion between God and human without distracting mediations was established. The previous exuberance for *quality times* – for feast days, processions, sacraments, blessings, sainthoods, pilgrimages, papal pardons, martyrdoms, rituals –

was quashed. All times became sacred. Or is that a paradox?

Likewise with secular notions that certain times are richer, more intensive and privileged than others. But surely (a perfectly responsible response would be) the year 2000 is *just* another year, a death or a triumph *just* events that happened but are now past. They bear no meaning. No time exudes more or less quality than any other time.

Modern-day, no-nonsense 'secular Protestants'; that is, economic rationalists, understand the situation clearly. Time simply moves, and all times are there to be used with equal efficiently. There is no natural 'time off', no 'Sabbath function'. Twenty-four-hours-a-day, seven-days-a-week service is the rational consequence: a limousine, a contraceptive, or a mortgage ready at all times. The 'happy hour' and the seasonal Sale are the only ghosts of *quality time* left.

What are we to believe? Is the choice between weighing the times or homogenising the times ultimately undecidable and unbridgeable? *Or, may it be the notion of a necessary choice that is the problem?* Instead of being forced to opt for one or the other we may need to consider both or neither. As Mircea Eliade reminds us, 'A tree, by virtue of the power it manifests, may become a blessed haven, without ceasing to be a tree' (Cirlot 1962). That a tree, or a piece of land, could be both sacred and secular, and all the confusing ramifications that follow, may be the lesson that certain people engaged in the current Australian debate on aboriginal land rights are unable or unwilling to concede.

So, what of the year 2000? It is special and will remain so for many because it has acquired meaning, and the creation and celebration of meaning are inseparable from being human. Some will be mesmerised by its apocalyptic call. Others will be touched by its sense of end and beginning and transition and new start. It can be easily seen as celebrating the anniversary of all births, of all deaths, of all resurrections, the occasion for the grandest trooping of the colors, a special time to look back and to look forward, to reflect on change and to wonder about continuity, the moment of and for history in its big sweep.

Yet at the same time, it is also transparently a product of the times. The actual millennium will in large part be shaped by the timely and untimely events that erupt at the time. We do not know which timely millennial quest or threat will announce itself and mark the occasion in quite specific ways. Nor do we know which untimely event, a death of a president, a military action, an economic collapse, will unexpectedly affect the actual event. All such secular phenomena will mingle with and color millennial *quality time*. And which will be which are indistinguishable. After all, a sacred tree remains a common plant that grows and eventually dies. And at no stage can we distinguish which bit of leaf, bark, or sap is the sacred bit and which is simply botanical.

The millennium to be experienced in the near future is not already there awaiting the moment of revelation; it will come packaged at the time, because it is produced on the spot by a complex global communication system. The millennium, like all events, will be a digest prepared. We will have to stomach something already methodically condensed, selected, processed, disposed, and dispersed. 'Artifactuality' is Derrida's term. The millennium we will experience will be, to simplify, a Murdoch millennium (the Rupert Murdoch, incidentally, who complained that 'people are paranoid about me'), or a Gates millennium. There is no unmediated 2000; it will be a filtered and filleted happening. It therefore has to be a Western phenomenon irrespective of anything else. This, of course, makes it no less real; it is just that its tragedy, glory, foolishness, or joy will come to us already highlighted and editorialised. The actual millennium will be 'meaning-full' on arrival.

So *quality time* is never pure. It always needs to accommodate human vicissitudes, but this does not weaken its significance. On the contrary.

When a person dies, it is not the end as some corporeal mass is buried or burned. For good or bad, a new archive is simultaneously opened, a new symbol, a new meaning is born. Another *quality time* (for some, not all) sets in, each taking its own form. Around the names of Marx and Freud no anniversary dates have ever crystallised and yet entire modes of thinking and living bear their names. And I write this on Bloomsday, June 16, 1998: the worldwide happening based on neither the birth nor death of author James Joyce, but on the fictitious day in 1904 on which his novel is set. It is not Irishness that is celebrated each year but as one commentator says, it is 'more about the experience of being human with all the colour, music and humour its author intended' (*The Age*, 16 July 1998).

Rational people, the Protestants in my tale (with apologies), are sound in many ways, but they simply deny our humanness, its foibles and its strengths, its necessity for meaning and value, and the very human nature for fantasy, hopes, fears, and exuberance. We cannot be purged of desires, any more than we can reasonably be commanded 'Thou shalt not lie'. It is these human attributes that inevitably create *quality times* for good and bad. A level playing field of time or of passion is inconceivable.

These putative secularists, however, are right in one way: *quality time* can occur at *any* time. I had such a moment the other day when I read the words of Angela Carter: 'Joyce never succumbed to the delusion that people who do not say complicated things do not have complicated thoughts' (*The Age*, 16 July 1998). How wise, I thought, and I hoped I would remember it until the end of time.

But *quality time* is a trickster that continues to tease and confound us simply because we are, ultimately, only human: we are driven to find meaning. So we 'find' it, again and again. Nothing, it seems, can be left unexplained. Any sense or reason or cause or significance we hungrily grasp, else we feel bereft, lost, and incomplete. This oh-so-human need for meaning regularly provokes the most primitive self-flagellation. In this regard, we are still of the thirteenth century.

But not everything 'has' meaning – whatever that verb entails. Not everything deserves such status: a tree may be just a tree, a pipe just a pipe, a day just a day. So, would it not be to our benefit to acquire a little more discipline, more discrimination, and more awareness in our choice and practice of *quality time*? And then just get on with 'being' and 'becoming' the rest of the time?

Who would orchestrate the new and improved archive? Who should? Remember, all *quality times* have a cost. And we always should be wary when appealed to 'in the name of —'.

But have we been carried away? Has *quality time* been given too high a profile? Made too special an experience? As if we have highlighted only the obvious—the visible tip of the iceberg—and assumed there is nothing more to note. Perhaps all that has been done is delineate the big bumps in an otherwise flat process of time. Nietzsche unintentionally gives us a clue that more may be involved.

He reminds us that we unwittingly commemorate, if not actually celebrate, dates painfully significant in our lives. Later, psychoanalysis is replete with stories of telling anniversary dates arousing anxiety, even pain, years after an emotional experience. But before the birth of that therapeutic practice, Nietzsche had already recorded his own experience of his father's death many years earlier:

> In the same year in which his life went downward, mine too, went downward: At thirtysix, I reached the lowest point of my vitality – I still lived, but without being able to see three paces ahead, spent the summer . . . like a shadow ... *The Wanderer and his Shadow* originated at this time. – At that time I knew about shadows ... (but) with every increase in vitality my ability to see has also increased again. (Nietzsche 1989)

Nietzsche's autobiography reminds us that we experience *quality times* at many levels of life, many of which we are unaware. Consciousness should never become the sole benchmark and focus of human behavior. Our lives are a mosaic of habits sculpted over time that we trot out again and again in response to life's repetitive calls, most of which we fail to notice – just moments, we assume, of reality, happening equally, evenly to us all. They are, however, stamped with their own particular quality, with their own special mix of heart and mind and gut. Every day we unwittingly 'celebrate', that is, relive, the 'anniversaries' of our past – not just our response to significant deaths and births, triumphs and traumas, or to grand dramas, but to private scenes and reminders of power, authority, conflict, love, envy, hate, fear, challenge, success, and failure – spectres that revisit us all. Each moment of our existence is another opportunity, another timely or untimely occasion, confronting us with our past, to once again 'identify' ourselves, to reaffirm what and who we are and need to be, for good or bad. Time is always the time of quality testing. Time is always the time when the (very) personal becomes the political, the intellectual, the artistic, and the everyday. So, the apparently banal, quotidian times of our life are also *quality times* in this fundamental and inevitable sense; and they follow their own rituals just as much as any visit to Las Vegas to relive the scene of an Elvis. We publicly remember the latter; we privately keep alive the former.

Quality time is therefore not, as we first suggested, the occasional highlight in an otherwise level playing field of time. The time of humans can never simply be a matter of quantity, of process, of duration. It is, irrevocably, one of quality, all the time. It is composed of bumps all the way; bumps on bumps, highs on already existing lows; lows on already existing highs, to return to an earlier image. In a way it is sacred all the time; it's just that some times are more sacred than others.

Chapter Three. Anticipating Future Time

A player of the calibre of John McEnroe, when he was at his peak, constantly thrilled his audience with strokes so perfectly timed that they appeared effortless and lethal – and it is this combination which regularly amazed spectators. They may at times have sensed that what contributed so effectively to this timing was an early preparation of his strokes. He seemed always already ready. It is, I suspect, only on few occasions that an admiring audience could see, and appreciate, what lay behind that: an ability, seemingly an uncanny one, to anticipate the play of the opponent. So uncanny sometimes that spectators came close to laughing, embarrassingly, at the supposed 'luck' of McEnroe as he managed not only to 'get the racket at' some extremely difficult or unexpected shot by the opponent, but then perchance to hit it for a winner. The wise audience 'knew' that only the exceptional player has such 'luck' and has it so often. It is uncanny.

Such a phenomenon is not restricted to sport. We see, at least sense it, in politics, business, strategic military planning, diplomacy and in the constant manoeuvres and countermanoeuvres of committee

– men, careerists, powerbrokers, and the otherwise innocents forced into such activity to defend their interests against the machinations of others. We all engage in anticipating. No mode of social life, however simple, exists without the regular operation of such future projections: we all have some idea how we will cope with the day's problems, or how friends are likely to react to an item of news. But the astute anticipate the future more successfully than the rest. Innocent parties are bewildered at what comes about unexpectedly or at how effectively they are out-manoeuvred by more astute colleagues or enemies who quietly position themselves to deliver an effortless but fatal *coup de grace*. Bloodless victories for some; unexpected, embarrassing defeat for others.

The dictionary helps us appreciate its many facets:

> prior action that 'prevents', provides for or precludes the action of another; assignment to too early a time, hence, observance in advance; occurrence in advance of the due time (hence in music) the introduction in advance of part of a chord which is to follow; intuitive preconception, a priori knowledge; the formation of opinions before examining the evidence; the action of realizing a thing before it occurs. (Shorter *OED*)

The French dictionary, *Le Petit Robert*, further embroiders:

a movement of thought which imagines or sees an event in advance; the anticipation of an act in advance; in literature, of anticipation such as fantasy which borrows from the supposed realities of the future. In economics, for example, a subjective hypothesis, either optimistic or pessimistic about the future which acts as a factor in economic fluctuations.

That anticipation is considered non-rational and nonlogical is emphasised by Chateaubriand: 'The heart anticipates the pains which menace it'. And it is not an attribute absolutely admired or encouraged. 'Let us not anticipate, let us not overtake events, let us respect the order and the succession of things'. We may misjudge the future or mistime the eventuality of things – thereby, mistaking the appropriate response. But we cannot stop from calculating the future, from forecasting what and when something may happen and, accordingly, from deciding what our best response ought to be.

Le Petit Robert reminds us of both sporting and wider applications; 'to forecast the reaction of the adversary and to prepare oneself to respond to it'. This is what talent is about. This is what we admire; what distinguishes the ultimate winners from the rest. Most associations have a positive ring, throwing up images of mental alertness, of being sensitively tuned to its environment, of possessing a fine sense of others' likely behaviour and predilections, of some intuitive notion of the probable consequence of things. Clearly beyond the rational, but qualities we normally admire, and often envy. But the notion is not limited to mental attributes; anticipation implies action, effective action. It combines prescience and intervention as well (and we normally infer the prescience from the intervention). The meaning in sport ('sensing the next reaction of the opponent and getting oneself ready to respond to it') captures it for most other activities as well. So, we are not dealing here with those people we may otherwise extol, such as a dreamer or a poet but, equally certainly, not with people who 'crash through or crash'.

Anticipation is refined activity. An exemplary perspicacity. And notice the 'social': we are not dealing here with some private psychology. Such an efficacious quality of anticipation is something we do not all possess in equal portion. On this count alone our personalities and talents differ. Are there cultural dispositions towards more or less 'anticipatory-skills' (to coin jargon)? The active, interventionist, practical, even instrumentalist quality of it could suggest it 'fits' certain popular images of the modern world, specifically the western world. At least one observer of the modern West, a Moroccan, Muhammad As-Saffar, Secretary to the Governor of Tetuan, as part of the first Moroccan embassy in Paris in 1845-6, was struck by this attribute. Of the French he wrote:

> They have no special strength in their bodies that others do not have; perhaps they are even weaker than others. But they have a concern for organi-

> sation and an aptitude for putting everything in its
> place. They construct all things on the firmest basis
> possible, and anticipate things before they happen
> (As-Saffar 1992: 121).

The French lack of physical strength, he believes, is compensated by their talent to look ahead, to see what is coming, and thereby to be prepared. To organise, to get things together in time, to be ready, and by such means acquire a strength one otherwise would not have. To anticipate, by disposition and training, increases one's power; it is a resource to call upon, an attribute overcoming otherwise superior oppositional forces. A deceptive, even gentle strength. To empower the otherwise weak.

Has As-Saffar pinpointed a western attribute – a confirmed inclination and talent to 'regard' the immediate future for signs of significant change, thereby being prepared to best cope with events as they emerge – and at the same time highlighted one of the West's strengths which has received little attention, in comparison with the talent for organisation so often remarked upon? The two complement each other: being prepared, in order, and anticipating eventualities, together constitute readiness and an efficient utilisation of time and other resources. A feedback is generated, almost a tautology – to organise means preparing in time for some future, anticipated eventuality. Have we come close, accidentally, to a neglected, major analytic of modernity?

But why do we not all equally utilise this potential? Some appear content to do nothing other than wait for events to erupt. Some, not others, are taken by surprise. But then, even if we learn to anticipate, nothing guarantees we read future signs correctly. And, even if we succeed in that goal, we are not always in a position to prepare ourselves appropriately. Are there prerequisites for the prerequisites? What is actually entailed in being ready?

What anticipation involves can be further appreciated by considering what it is not. *Le Petit Robert* provides two antonyms. One is *différer*, to defer. To put off, to postpone, to hold over. The decision not to act or to intervene for the moment. A psychology of deferring points to notions like ambivalence, uncertainty, doubt, hesitation, fear, anxiety. If anticipation emphasises positive moves, even if premature, this opposite highlights their absence, a postponement of intervention. But perhaps we have moved too fast and anticipated too rashly. Deferring is not necessarily an antonym of anticipating – the one holding back, the other projecting forth. A deferment may be the anticipation's actual outcome. We may positively decide to postpone doing something because we anticipate that to do otherwise would lead to error or some other undesired outcome. A decision not to act is still, as Gregory Bateson reminded us, a decision. Just as a non-response may well be a response, and a responsible response, as Derrida has helped us see.

Anticipation, in other words, encompasses an intricate and subtle range of initiatives. We ought not to restrict it to images of decisive interventions catching others by surprise. Anticipation goes beyond the split-second recovery and amazing physical alertness of a John McEnroe at the net. It may include the tactical retreat before an expected enemy offensive; even a fortifying drink before an 'inevitable' confrontation; or a judicious decision to postpone, again, that talk with the boss. So 'defer' needs qualification: it need not be anticipation's contrary.

The second antonym is *revenir* (*sur*): to retract, go back on, hark back to, to retrace, crop up again. Here the opposition is more temporal in its bearing. Where anticipation is forwardlooking (in time), *revenir* conjures up going or looking back. Forms of repetition. And in that sense, also 'negative', like deferral.

The two set of associations conjure up Freud. The first, to return to the same – the repetition compulsion; the second, to again postpone – the constipation of ambivalence, of crippling doubt. Pathologies of human behaviour. No longer is the actor alert and in charge of his future, anticipating others and timing responses accordingly – rather the person is acted upon, being in no way in control of his or her destiny. Notions of timing fade, as do any ideas of a future. Instead, the individual remains a prisoner of either the past, regularly revisited, or the present, constantly unable to surrender. The contrast seems sharp – but is it?

One may, for example, be alert to the future, ever ready to step in and alter the course of things and yet still be tied to the past. Indeed, the degree of repetition compulsion we all experience goes a long way in preparing us to face the future – in roughly the same way every time. Responses are patterned, not different each time. The need of repetition, in other words, is as much a thing in front of us as behind. It shapes what we are likely to do in response to events undreamt at any moment. We are, in a way, 'caught' each time by a disposition to anticipate optimistically or pessimistically, rashly, prematurely, over-defensively, in a paranoid fashion, cautiously, or aggressively. Done well or not, it will, to some degree, repeat how we have always done it. A skill or disability in timing is not something constantly varying for each of us; on the contrary, overtime we hone and perfect our particular style, admirable or not. The past and future are again shown not to be the obvious opposites our language and conventional thinking encourage us to expect.

Even the notion of deferral is linked to forms of anticipation. Freud's understanding of the operations of the unconscious undermines conventional notions of causality and time – the two being linked overtime. The 'scene of writing' is such that actions are not triggered at the time of their 'first' cause (or indeed, their 'latest' cause), that is, when we would commonly expect them to occur; they are deferred for future occasions when they are called up again from our inerasable memory, the 'mystic writing-pads' to use Freud's imagery (Freud 1925). So, our actions of anticipation are less reactions to some future foreseen event than reactions of some deferred past. Our allegedly keen prescience may be more an unavoidable reminiscence. We anticipate by *déjà vu*. To pre-see what is coming may well be a timely warning, but the chain of causality is not expected; the 'warning' we receive is that from another time and the coincidence of the times. We are moved by a timely reminder. By such a coincidence we ready ourselves to face the future by facing the past. There is little difference; each helps to constitute the other. McEnroe honed his skill by constant practice over time.

So once again, what we commonly take as exclusive oppositions turn out to be necessary elements of each other. To anticipate, to defer and to hark back to are not so much separate, let alone contrary motions, but distinctive aspects of each other without which none can exist. Each being a requisite part of the other we can no longer say that the past causes the present, or that the present causes the future. The linearity of time collapses. What remains is timing, successful or otherwise, and that has no direction, spatial or temporal. Despite the rigour and authority with which physicists and biologists like Stephen Hawkins and Ilya Prigogine defend the traditional notion of irreversible time, and which gets supported by our commonsense, a strong case exists for rejecting that belief in favour of one awkwardly characterised by both or neither reversibility and irreversibility. The intricacies of anticipation force such a redefinition.

And another common-sense supports this change. To anticipate an event does not, however, necessarily highlight timing. Whether something is likely to occur today, tomorrow or next month may be irrelevant compared to the specificity of the thing expected. One may dread the event or feel euphoric about it irrespective of its due date. In anticipation we often fantasise about a future; one that we live over and over again – psychologically, even physically. The future is present. And when it finally comes we may experience a shock of the real. An athlete was asked, after the women's marathon of the Barcelona Olympic Games, about the horrors of the Montjuic hill; 'the anticipation was worse than it was', the Australian bronze medalist replied. The article continued, with welcome irony: 'For Australians, the outcome of the Olympic women's marathon was exactly the opposite. The anticipation was so much better than the result'. That is, emotions also enter the scene; they contribute as well to our future scenarios. We invest in the future, at times heavily. Thus we have our fears, suspicions, paranoias as well as our day-dreams of glory, and our secret rehearsals of handling that expected moment of triumph or embarrassment or pathos. We may dread the future we are convinced we are about to witness; in pain we experience it before its time. We may exalt the coming moment of glory. The banal reality when it finally arrives can be disconcerting. To many athletes, Montjuic hill was a pleasant surprise on the day. 'Let us anticipate, let us

Ellingsen in *Watching the Windsors come apart*, where he argued that the pattern was set up in 1968 when BBC TV was allowed unprecedented access to the private world of the monarchy. The film *Royal Family* then attracted an audience of 22 million. It had nothing to say about the royals' personal lives, but opened up to the public gaze an institution that had long been shielded. Ellingson reported that what *Royal Family* did provide 'was the context in which their later misdemeanours would be judged and this meant that the public was 'conceptually ready' – even if the royals were not – for pictures of the Duchess of York topless in St Tropez' (Ellingsen *The Age*, 29 May 2001).

Anticipating the future is obviously chancy and easy to get wrong. As distinct, presumably, from knowing the past. But Robert Grudin, for one, questions whether 'hindsight', yet another apparent antonym of anticipation, is all that it's cracked up to be:

The ironic phrase 'wisdom of hindsight', meaning an opinion after the event which is correct but futile, is based on the almost universal assumption that we know more about things after they have happened than before...There are reasons for doubting that this assumption is completely justifiable. After an event, we normally know at most what happened; not what might have happened, had one or more of its innumerable circumstances been altered. What we 'understand' in other words, is the result of a single configuration of variables, rather than the sum of what these variables were capable of producing. And we understand each circumstance only in the sense in which, conjoined with others, it produced the happening, rather than in terms of its full potentialities. Moreover, deluged in details, we miss the nobler and simpler view of forms and purposes we had when looking into the future. Finally, the fact that retrospective analyses, as opposed to prior strategies and predictions, hold little danger (they need only be plausible) often renders us more careless and self-indulgent in making them (Gudrin 1997: 61-2).

However, anticipation is not, as we have seen, the innocent opposite of retrospective study. And 'carelessness and self-indulgence' intrude anywhere: in a hasty anticipation of the past as in an impulsive forearming for some future. Kundera reminds us how easily we slip into facile interpretation:

Man proceeds in a fog. But when he looks back to judge people, he sees no fog on their path. From his present, which was their far away future, their path looks perfectly clear to him, good visibility all the way. Looking back he sees the path, he sees the people preceding, he sees their mistakes, but not the fog. And yet all of them—Heidegger, Mayakovski, Aragon, Ezra Pound—were all walking in fog, and one might wonder: who is more blind?—Mayakousky's blindness is part of the eternal human condition. But for us not to see the fog on Mayakousky's path is to forget what man is, forget what we ourselves are (Kundera 1996).

We easily 'forget what we ourselves are' – as we forget

that our past is not something simply left behind us. We may even forget what the future holds and demands, because our human time is not grammatically tensed. To construe or misconstrue the one bears heavily on the appreciation of the other. Our ability to anticipate is not temporally anchored to the future; it is diffuse and general. Derrida exemplifies this well when, at the time of Louis Althusser's funeral, he warns against premature misjudgments of that author and calls for patience in understanding his times and its possibilities:

> I dream of addressing those who come after him, or after us already, and whom I see (alas, by several signs) as too much in a hurry to understand, to interpret, to classify, fix, reduce, simplify, close off and judge, that is, to misunderstand that, here, it is a question of an oh-so-singular destiny and that the trials of existence, of thought, of politics, inseparably. I would ask them to stop a moment, to take the time to listen to our time (we had no other one), to patiently decipher everything that from our time could be ratified and promised in the life, the work, the name of Louis Althusser (Derrida 2003: 117)

And Derrida urges this care not only because 'this destiny should demand respect' but also 'because the yet open wounds, the scars or hopes, will certainly teach them something essential of what remains to be heard, read, thought and done'. We best anticipate the future and know what can and should be done, the better we know the past'.

So, anticipation should not be seen as a simple matter of speed, but as readiness. To anticipate is not to 'go off halfcocked,' but to know something in advance and accordingly, to be appropriately prepared. Once again, a simple linear notion of time misleads. Acting prematurely, precipitately, is nothing more than a question of 'length of time' – being faster or earlier which can result in being too fast or too early – or just too wrong. Anticipation, on the other hand, is a question of quality, of timing, of being so appropriately prepared that one 'meets' what is coming. Derrida seems to have something like this in mind when, in another work, he distinguishes anticipation from precipitation: 'To anticipate is to take the initiative, to be out in front, to take (*capere*) in advance (*ante*). Different from precipitation, which exposes the head (*prae-caput*), the head first and ahead of the rest, anticipation would have to do with the hand.' To talk appreciatively of anticipation, and appropriate readiness, rests on a specific notion of time. It is that some form of repetition rather than linear newness forms time. If we were destined to experience nothing but constant originality we would hardly bother considering the question of timing. Under such circumstances, whether we timed an event well or badly would be entirely arbitrary. We would exist in an environment of constant surprise and chance. A life dictated by nothing other than the permanent 'shock of the new'

would hardly engender human curiosity about the

qualities of timeliness.

If time were an exact duplication of a past we would be little concerned about our various states of preparedness. We would long past have mastered the one, required key; life would contain no surprises. Only when time reproduces a form of repetition which is the same yet different are we motivated to consider the idea of timing. We learn from what has happened already, but that learning can never provide the answers, because no answer exists. At best we can prepare to be ready. We can anticipate, with knowledge, skill and luck, and meet the future as best we can.

Cultures are as much future investments as they are past treasures, Derrida argues in his 'reflections on today's Europe'. They anticipate their 'becoming' as much as celebrating their 'being' or what 'they once were'. And, in anticipating, they have always two choices, both of which they have to follow to some degree, Derrida continues.

> All cultures have some identifiable telos, both a memory and a promise which they need to persist in anticipating. A telos is in no way 'once and for all', 'given' and 'identifiable in advance'. So, what is in part anticipatable is the 'unanticipatable', the 'non-identifiable', 'that of which one does not yet have a memory' (Derrida 1992: 17).

A danger to any culture, he says, lurks in both necessities. We need to be 'suspicious' of complacent and deadening 'repetitive memory'; but likewise suspicious of the 'absolutely new', 'the surprising, the virginal and the unanticipatable' because 'We know the "new" only too well, or in any case the old rhetoric, the demagogy, the psychology of the "new"—and sometimes of the "new order".'

The dilemma has no simple answers; resorting to a rule of thumb is irresponsible. So much depends on the time and timing. Each answer must be related to which 'today' is being considered. Derrida constantly stresses the importance of contingency. Each time we anticipate we are at risk of the future; but responsibility begins with appreciating both the 'double-binds' within which we need to operate.

Thus for instance, to learn from the example of Althusser 'something essential of what remains to be heard, read, thought and done'. Derrida ends his funeral oration with Althusser's words:

> We eat the same bread, experience the same angers, the same revolts, the same deliria, – not to mention the same despondency over a time that no History can move. Yes, like Mother Courage, we have the same war on our doorstep, a hairsbreadth away, even inside us, the same horrible blindness, the same ashes in our eyes, the same earth in our mouths. We possess the same dawn and the same night: our unconsciousness. We share the same story – and that is where everything begins. (Derrida 2003).

This is where we begin. This is where we begin to feel

the future.

Chapter Four. To Play with Time

Can we conceive a new knowledge, politics and ethics more suited to transient time – to know and use the moment and the occasion no matter how fleeting? But something beyond a vulgar opportunism. We will need more subtle distinctions – of time and of behaviour – than we are accustomed to. But can we break away from our entrenched attraction to enduring principles? From long-term quests? From immemorial causes like the valiant struggle against evil and the endless triumphant crusades of goodness? We love to be seduced by eternal time. But we pay a price which we commonly fail to notice. If only for the moment, let us suspend conventional judgments and contemplate an alternative. Let's flirt. Let's risk uncertainty. And our technique, just for the occasion? A series of swift raiding parties not a sustained campaign of reasoned argument.

Early in his book *Heidegger, Art and Politics*, Philippe Lacoue-Labarthe notes as an aside that Heidegger was by no means alone in what he did.

> Who in this century... whether of 'right' or 'left' of the various revolutionary projects, has not been

duped? And in the name of what? ... What of those who were great figures in their respective ways? I cite at random Hansum, Benn, Pound, Blanchot, Drieu and Brasillach ... Or, in the other camp, Benjamin, Brecht, Bataille, Malraux ... What did the old world have to offer them with which they could have resisted the irruption of the so-called 'new world'? (Lacoue-Labarthe, 1990: 21-2).

The word 'duped' points the way, suggesting being led astray from some assumed norm, say, of careful thought. It suggests cunning and manipulative persuasion. Nor does duped imply being bought by vulgar bribes; although it may witness the power of flattery and its psychological procurements. [Casanova's credo for seduction was 'praise the beautiful for their intelligence, and the intelligent for their beauty'.]

'Duped', however, seems misleading because it suggests too passive a role. They were not victims but active participants; complicit one way or other in what was being done. Nor hoodwinked against their will, they embraced their own seduction.

Let's momentarily step back. Don Giovanni, in Mozart's opera, fascinates. We are drawn to him again and again. He repels as he appeals. Rather, we periodically think we should be repelled, but we find it hard to make up our minds. We take him as the great lover, as a Casanova. We envy him. But we also know there looms a dark side to the man. It is not simply that he is a feckless seducer of women or even a murderer. We are disconcerted by his remarkable power over people. But we appreciate his wit, resourcefulness, risk-taking, his unwillingness to surrender or to repent even in the face of death. We can ignore neither his charms nor his admirable persistence. All this is possibly the clue. *To be what he is as Don Giovanni is to be all these things at the same time.* His diverse qualities complement not contradict each other. To be seductive he cannot have one without the other. Our ambivalence is appropriate.

The opera is not a study of evil versus good, of a tyrant and his victims; it is more a work which undermines certainties arising out of simple oppositions. It alerts us to the untidiness of reality, to the danger of making categoric judgments about human affairs, including the apparently horrid. It also alerts us to our own complicities in the work of others. In judging them we are unwittingly judging ourselves. Don Giovanni exemplifies an 'uncertainty principle': the more we know of human detail the more uncertain we are of categoric truths; the less we know of its complexities the more certain we are of the Truth.

This 'message' is the opera's content and form. We experience the ambiguity with all its attractions and doubts. Along with Donna Elvira, Zerlina, Leporello and others, we are seduced by the opera. We may even quietly wish to be seduced; so, we often suppress the Don's unsavouriness. The opera is ultimately not a simple story of serial sexuality; *it is a portrayal of the insidious, intricate and pervasive seductiveness of seduction.*

Don Giovanni is not in pursuit merely of sexual satisfaction. He is more concerned to experience again and again his control over the minds, souls and bodies of others. He is driven to endlessly repeat such 'total' conquests, over male or female. Never satisfied, never quite certain, he is compelled to test and retest his skills. As his conquests return again and again to repeat their abjection, driven to be seduced as much as he seems driven to seduce.

The opera ends with ironic declarations that the evil Giovanni, pulled down to hell, got what he deserved. Impervious to the fact that they themselves had previously got what they deserved as well. No one is an innocent victim in seduction – which distinguishes it from naked power or rape. We tend to deny this quality. Still today we take deceptive comfort simply with the destruction of the 'evil party'.

Don Giovanni shows little appreciation of reality – or is he disturbingly correct in his understanding of human behaviour? He is narcissistic: his reality is only that of his own construction, his fantasy that he can always do whatever he wants to. He cannot tolerate frustration; a viciousness quickly erupts. He has no past, no specific future; only an ever- present present. The success of the moment his sole concern, his perverse self-gratification. Only his rules are relevant.

What aids the seducer, often against the odds, is his transparent faith in himself. Of his ability to win he is certain. He suffers neither doubt nor hesitation. And it seems infectious to those around him. We observers have less certainty. We can never quite make up our minds about the worth of narcissism: a healthy autonomy or a selfish disregard for others?

In all these ways the seducer's behaviour is predictable. He seems compelled to repeat. Yet one thing inevitably introduces uncertainty into an otherwise reliable scenario. Giovanni, with his commitment to seduction, is not only powerless to prevent the most unexpected responses, but actually promotes them. It is not a matter of chance interventions.

His unrestrained behaviour triggers extreme consequences. What unfolded was never certain. Yet, should anyone have been surprised? Ultimately no-one was in control. Excess prompts excess, just as Elvira tells us: 'In what excesses, oh ye gods, in what dreadful, horrible crimes, is this wretch steeped! Heaven's wrath cannot be deferred ... By your wiles ... you managed to seduce my heart, you made me love you ... If he does not return I'll tear out his heart'. Once convention is seriously breached, anything can result. Seduction can never be taken lightly.

Parallels between Don Giovanni and Lacoue-Labarthe's intellectuals are many. Let me just briefly refer to a few of these. Rational persuasion is quite irrelevant. One believes or does not believe in the big picture – you are seduced or you are not – that is all. And, if you are not, it is likely because you are already seduced elsewhere. You cultivate certainty in one place or another. But for all the certainty of goals, extreme and unpredictable events can traumatically erupt.

The advent of hypnotism in the 19th century, Adam Phillips recently suggested, exposed, just how lowbrow people really were. It wasn't truth or goodness they were after: they wanted to be moved ... The hypnotist removes inhibition, and releases talent, but in doing this he enslaves a person to his will – an extreme description of what every parent, teacher, doctor and political leader does (and knows he does). [It] inevitably leads us to wonder – *whether seducing and being seduced is actually all we are free to do.* (Phillips, 2000: 8-10, my emphasis)

The willing behaviour of even the most intelligent people during the great ideological clashes was not peculiar. What of the present-day, worldwide, mass seductions under the sway of national, ethnic, religious identifications? Of the seemingly irresistible pull of honour, face, pride, true faith, free-world, globalising, free-marketing world, a world to be saved from human recklessness, order, liberation, progress? What of love? Hate? Consider these lines:

> If we must die – oh, let us nobly die,
> So that our precious blood may not be shed
> In vain; then even the monsters we defy
> Shall be constrained to honour us though dead.
> (Claude McKay, *If We Must Die* in Nkosi, 2000: 30)

Winston Churchill quoted this to the US Congress in his effort to obtain American commitment in the Second World War. He prudently failed to acknowledge the source – a poem written in the 1920s by the black,

Claude McKay, when rabid lynch mobs roamed the American South. The seductiveness and calls of seduction are readily transferable. The finest causes may rub shoulders with the vilest. The qualities of seduction are there in all instances.

Not unlike the case of Don Giovanni, we are both attracted and repelled by such seductions. To fight unstintingly for freedom, to face any sacrifice, to persist whatever the odds, are not only considered honourable, they are emotionally gratifying. The psychic rewards of being seduced are many and deep.

To be swept up by a seduction brings pleasure as much as pain. The dedication called upon is compensated by the joy of belonging. One is carried along as if on the side of Time. That heady feeling of effortless efficacy, that irrepressible feeling of true freedom and full certainty.

It is not accidental that Don Giovanni ends in a violent death. He is not simply pulled down to hell by the ghost, he leaps to his death unrepentent. Death not life seems a common, final quality of seduction. Seductive death. Its triumphant end. No wonder warfare is the most potently charged symbol of seduction. Deep down the time of seduction seems ultimately irreversible – from life to death.

Yet an ambivalence persists. Instead of praise we may ridicule; instead of crowning another hero we may identify another fool or villain – willing to sacrifice life, his and others. The Faustian tragedy seems inexorably associated with seduction. The more carried away with some myth of righteous certainty the more easily one succumbs to the allurements of ploys and promises guaranteeing ultimate success, at whatever cost.

Not surprisingly there has been an abiding public imagery of the 'mad scientist'. The quest for great scientific truths and for the power, for good or bad, awaiting those who attain them, has long marked Science as one of the West's great seductions. Nothing but 'genome hysteria' says a respected geneticist of the ethical debate on bio-technology; 'most scientists entered the field for altruistic reasons', he insists (quoted by Douez, 2001: 8). He is of course missing the point, for that is the point. As another geneticist recently commented 'the seductive power, potentially, of genetic engineering is so great that society will do it ... The concern is that good people, meaning to do good things ... [will] slip down a slippery slope' (quoted by Ellingsen, 2001: 13).

The appeal of certainty can even appear poignant, if not pathetic. An eminent biologist contrasts science to the many historical scams 'desperately seeking certainty' (the unintentionally ironic title of his article):

Science is special ... Unlike other belief systems those of science are universal and culture-free ... Believe it or not, most of physics and chemistry, and even ... biology, is right, and will remain there forever. Lucretius ... should have been referring to science when he so perceptively remarked: 'Happy the man who knows the causes of things' (Wolpert, 2001: 4).

Do we have to succumb to some seductiveness or other? Are there no other options? Forget reason. Think of something with more appeal and efficacy.

Why does flirtation get such a bad press? The case against it is rarely articulated – there apparently is no need; we all know the line. It is, they say, insincere, irresponsible, childish, immature, fickle, heartless. It treats people, ideas and causes with casual disdain, with cynicism. Nothing is valued. And we can hardly conceive of value without some degree of commitment there, some loyalty, endurance, upholding principle. Flirting is also unreliable and flighty. It is what 'mature man' is not. Flirtation may well be a bit of fun – but so are all childish games. Ultimately we call for commitment, a firm belief in something beyond a passing fancy. Mere dalliance records low on our morality-counter. Sincerity is called for.

But how sincere is our common idea of sincerity? To be sincere: 'pure, unmixed, free from any foreign element or ingredient, genuine, unadulterated, exact, veracious; not falsified or perverted in any way, containing no element of dissimulation or deception, straightforward' (*Oxford English Dictionary*). This is hardly a useful description of humanity. More than an ideal, it is a fantasy. A self-deception we secretly covet.

Besides, if for a moment we were to follow conventional thoughts on sincerity and commitment would we not have to include Hitler, Stalin, Mao, Reagan, Thatcher among its finest exemplars?

Let's reframe the phenomenon. Flirtation is an end in itself, not a means to some other end. In fact, it negates ends. At the least it defers them, endlessly, open-ended. It eschews conclusions, and so is independent of commitment involving duration of time in pursuit of a goal. It is true that in popular imagery we 'commit' ourselves only to the long haul, never to the fleeting action. Nevertheless it may well be, as Phillips says of monogamy that 'one is only ever really faithful to fidelity itself, never merely one's partner' (1996: 33). What we so often admire may therefore be little more than commitment to commitment. Nietzsche long ago suggested that the western demand for certainty 'stems from mere timidity and extreme insecurity' (Vitiello, 1996: 151).

Flirtation, unlike commitments such as seduction, is the expression of a desire for adventure, excitement, novelty; the thrill of a challenge, even a certain provocative self-torment – it is tantalising. The process itself is the desired product. Means and ends condense.

Flirtation is full of surprises as it deliberately seeks the unfamiliar. It plays with time; a strategy of chance and change in a mutable world. It is another world view, one denying linear time, progress, duration, regularity, stability, order and wholeness. Its orientation is anti-stasis, anti-status-quo, anti-stability. Flirtation is constant movement, the unavoidable creativity of 'permanent revolution'. Flirts are never satisfied because they do not seek 'satisfaction as culmination'. Like Lord Krishna of the Hindu pantheon, to flirt with flirting is all. Georg Simmel, like Krishna, recognised the fatal impact of resolution: 'Every conclusive decision brings flirtation to an end' (Phillips, 1994: xxi).

Flirtation is of the moment; an engagement no doubt, but a transcient one, a passing affair. As life itself – remember Venerable Bede's depiction of the 'life of man': 'As if when on a winter's night… a single sparrow should fly swiftly into the hall, and coming in at one door, instantly fly out through another… it is lost to your eyes' (Griffiths, 2000: 258).

In the essay 'On Transcience', Freud criticises those who place value only on long-term, life-and-death matters – rather than on the fleeting pleasures and beauty of passing moments (Freud, 1916: 303-10). This may be what the unidealised life is all about. But the dominant western tradition persistently privileges long time over short time, structure over event, permanance over change. Interestingly, Freud elsewhere dismisses 'American flirtation' as 'shallow and empty' compared to 'a continental love-affair'. That the cherry-blossom soon wilts and dies, that a happening quickly disappears, that humans can never guarantee immortality, nothing proclaims their inherent inferiority. Why does the West overvalue length and demean 'ephemeral matters'?

Flirtation is flirting with uncertainty, not as an

unfortunate outcome, but as a cultivation of the indefinite. It encourages chance to set the scene; one just takes it up and runs with it. Chance prohibits its plotting. It just happens and one either seizes the opportunity – readiness counts – or loses it. That is why photography is considered the most flirtatious of all the arts: 'pure contingency and can be nothing else', Barthes says (1982: 15). Seizing the chance is a matter of good timing. The auspicious moment – a notion enlightened modernity prefers to ignore.

Flirtation highlights timing not time. To flirt is to operate on the callings of the times; some occasions are opportune; others not. Flirting takes the opportunities which offer themselves. So flirting is occasional – from time to time: you neither plan it, hunt it, fabricate it. You are merely ready each time it presents itself; but 'readiness' may be everything (a critical notion).

With seduction on the other hand you feel a virginal commitment to its very idea. 'This is It': a once-in-a-lifetime feeling. And a certain egoism: you have been chosen; your time has come. And it will be forever.

Denial is a busy business. Preoccupied with the ruses of escape. Always ready to be distracted, led astray, away from the duties and difficulties of life, and as T.S. Eliot observed: 'human kind cannot bear very much reality'. So it may seem is flirtation – a dalliance, 'a diversion of the mind or attention – usually in an adverse sense', says the *Oxford*.

But language itself can distract – can lead us away from looking freshly at convention. 'To distract', the *Oxford* tells us, 'to draw away from fatiguing or serious occupations; to entertain or amuse'. Flirtation, in this view, can be nothing other than a momentary escape from the real tasks at hand. A descent in the moral order.

However, if reality is characterised by chance, change and contingency we can reevaluate matters. Seduction, as any long-term preoccupation, we can now see, acts as a defence against the actual contingencies of reality. And consequently, against the task of flirting, of coping, with this mobile, transient world. But we fear the uncertainties of chance so deny its dominant role in life. Even the planning of ideals can be tyrannical. Hear Adam Phillips on success:

> Our ambitions – our ideals and success stories that lure us into the future – can too easily become ways of not living in the present, a blackmail of distraction; ways, that is, of disowning, or demeaning, the actual disorder of experience. Believing in the future can be a great deadener. Perhaps we have been too successful at success and failure, and should now start doing something else. (Phillips, 1994: 58)

And as Phillips argues elsewhere, 'Flirtation may not be a poor way of doing something better, but a different way of doing something else' (Phillips, 1994: xxii).

The writer John O' Donohue honours poets because he sees them as 'utterly dedicated to the threshold where language and silence meet [and] who strive to be faithful to uncertainty'. A flirt likewise turns his or her back on certainty – it kills all manner of creativity. Flirtation is the threshold where pasts confront potential futures. It is a Janus-moment of curiosity, open-endedness, change. The challenge and excitement of uncertain times.

Flirtation is therefore best seen as play; not a game, that demands strict rules. Play is free-play, free association, and valorised, as if by a Nietzsche. Play is disrupted by obligations and solemnity. W.H. Auden found it 'a little irritating' the way even 'the very greatest artists ... [would] think themselves important ... To be able to devote one's life to art without forgetting that art is frivolous is a tremendous achievement ... Shakespeare never takes himself too seriously'. Shakespeare was a flirt. Auden continues: 'major writers [are] ... always trying something new and not caring if it fails, like Shakespeare, Picasso and Wagner ... the minor writer works on one masterpiece with the idea of bringing it to perfection' (Auden, quoted by Kermode, 2001: 11).

Being in thrall to perfection preconditions seductive engagement. On the other hand, to be uncertain forecloses grandiosities of goals, unquestioned devotion and a certain narcissism. Seduction eschews novelty and fears the eruptions of contingency. Flirtations hardly crystallise into monuments for others to idealise. Play is unrepresentable, a matter of the present. (We know however the ways of routinisation, of the seductions of order and ossified representation taking over. A critical term one day becomes a catchy phrase tomorrow, and then a cliché, a brand name the next. 'Guernica' is currently a classy Melbourne restaurant.)

Our moorings may be more fragile than we admit. Even when unwilling to forego all current rewards we may entertain traces of longings elsewhere. Complete, unquestioned satisfaction seems doomed never to be a human quality. Something is always missing; some lack a persistent irritant. Vincenzo Vitiello tells us that all Greek tragedy contemplates absence. 'The absence of God. Dionysus is not there. He is never there ... And it is this that makes all certainty uncertain, all quiet disquiet ... The tragic chorus does not calm things, but quite the opposite: it heightens the disquiet' (Vitiello, 1996: 152). Can we ever experience complete certainty, complete satisfaction? It is not surprising that from time to time we change track even if only in the privacy of our personal fantasies.

I experienced a shift just then. I now realise I was being driven to present the case for flirtation in a manner more fitting to seduction; attempting to cover all problems comprehensively; to leave no room for doubt. I was seduced away from flirting with flirtation in the name of the greater certainties of reasoned, academic persuasion. But this should not be the time for the last word on it. A love-poem is not diminished by failing to cover all that passion's habits.

Our understandings are always partial and we remain more plural than singular no matter the commitment. Do I know (could I know) what you – or I – even mean by uncertainty? Is it hesitation and doubt or open-ended curiosity or what? Does it vary without our awareness? Our engagements always carry risks. As Adam Phillips argued: 'everything we say is an experiment because we can never be quite sure how people will react, or how we ourselves will react' (Phillips, 1996: 90). When Heisenberg returned to Germany after his talks with Bohr in Copenhagen in 1941 was he able to distinguish his physics from his politics as he pursued the German war effort? And did he learn, for certain, what love of country means? Was his failure to make 'certain calculations' at that time due to his incompetence or, rather, to some 'unconscious reluctance' if, as Michael Frayn wonders, 'what he was trying to do was not to build a bomb' (Frayn, 1998: 112). We can never know.

A certain aesthetic of Alexander Nehamas further unsettles rigid distinctions between seduction and flirtation. Judgments of taste, he says, are ultimately guesses.

> We find things beautiful... when we sense we haven't exhausted them... Beauty is the enemy of certainty... [and] is a constant reminder that the value of life itself is a disputable matter... The return of the beautiful is welcome because it intimates a new willingness to acknowledge our love of uncertainty, and the uncertainty of love (Nehamas, 2000: 26).

Could the experience of the beauty of life seduce us one day to love uncertainty and its flirtations?

'Have I been understood?', I am tempted to ask, after Nietzsche (1989: 333). Metaphors are risky things – but so are concepts. 'Seduction' and 'flirtation' need to be handled gingerly. Treat them too seriously or for too long and they lose their value – a use of language is also an abuse of language, Heidegger once warned.

This speculative foray is little more than an initial reconnoitre. The purpose is limited: to suggest that despite the many tragedies associated with historical seductions, the West has morally sanctioned that type of attachment more than those seen as its opposite. I want to question that cultural heritage. Can we conceive of a new knowledge: one fitting more, for example, Neitzsche's hope that the historian of the future will be brave enough to say 'perhaps'; or Paul Feyerabend's final plea 'against method': 'the life we lead is ambiguous ... I want you to remember ... especially when the story seems to become so definite that it almost turns into a clearly thought-out and precisely structured point of view' (Feyerabend, 2000: 28). Can we think of a new politics, way of life, morality – which Derrida urges us – one more suitable to a reality, as I see it, of chance, uncertainty, transcience and paradox? Can we conceive a relevant ethics which is not, nevertheless, just an excuse for opportunism? Fine tuning is called for because they can look so much like each other: the times seem the same, for example – brief, sudden, arbitrary.

An answer may appear to lie in simple compromise, a mere matter of good timing: sometimes call for seduction, others for flirtation; we can do without neither. That approach has appeal. However, such an option still exposes us to the terrors and the atrophy of seduction.

Flirtation's uncertainties may best help forge a new ethics more appropriate to singularities (being both idiosyncratic and exemplary) rather than relying on one timeless ethic. An 'ethics of the event' to supplement the 'mathesis singularis' of Barthes. Again, it is a matter of timing, but one far more complex than a choice between simple alternatives. Slajov Žižek's idea of the 'structural impossibility of "society"' seems related to my 'structural uncertainty of existence', both obliging us always to act against seemingly insurmountable constraints. But to attend to human paradox can never mean further rules, laws, codes. We have been there. The daunting task now is constant reinvention without the comfort of conclusive answers. Intellectuals should be flirts – it is their responsibility. And others? Will most continue to be seduced by the recognised pleasures and putative safety of seduction? I don't know.

Part Two

Two Views of Timing

Chapter Five. Political Time - a matter of timing.

When P. became deputy leader last year, it appeared that only time stood between him and the leadership... But now...

He's a genius, a supreme strategist. He uses time as an absolute tool: he has taught me how you can let something happen simply by manipulating your timing a bit. You can let a thing self-destruct; you don't have to destroy it. Or you can get the maximum out of something by pacing yourself.

The time for a consumption tax's introduction is now past...

Too little too late, or too much too soon? His chance is gone. That is, unless...

(extracts, made anonymous, from *The Age* newspaper, Melbourne, 1992).

One particular time appears to receive little attention. Provisionally, and for reasons which will emerge, I call it 'political time'. We first may note some connection with the symptom of simultaneity, events occurring together in time. But *political time* entails some sequential ordering as well; it exists over time, encompassing some complexity of events. It constitutes, as it were, a period of history, be that a matter of days, weeks, months or longer; but, as we discover here, there is no unequivocal start or end or duration. What occurs during this sequence, and to it, is of supreme importance to the study, let alone to actors involved. *Political time* is an essay in human endeavour and a consideration of its efficacy.

Political time is the operation of timing and the question of timeliness, of good or bad timing; of the juxtaposition of times: those humanly engineered with that of the passage and nature of times as they eventuate, erupt or dissipate as they may. It is concerned with what can and cannot be achieved in the pursuit of some desire: with the intervention and the response, the initiated and the obligatory, pre-emptions taken and superventions rallied. It is an exercise in managing auspicious times and in avoiding or modifying inauspicious times, a consideration of the many qualities in human perspicacity, sensitivity, cunning, manipulation and orchestration. It is also, necessarily, the study of chance, luck, fortune; of the unexpected, the unforeseeable; of the opportune and the unwelcome.

Political time is a constantly shifting and elusive play between chance and necessity (there is a voluminous literature on the surprising similarity of necessity and chance). Its potential range of movement is wide. An event of *political time* may appear totally arbitrary; or it may appear over-determined; or again by its uncertain quality it may challenge our conventional distinction between chance and determinism, and force us to reconsider where the boundary between these two poles actually lies. We may begin to sense that some necessity lurks within the apparently most random event, or that the thing seemingly most determined nevertheless contains an element of chance.

Political time is also a study of fortunes as they engage with the times; and of this confrontation being used or misused by the endeavours of concerned actors. Can one enhance the opportunity of the moment? Can one counter an unfortunate turn of events? Whichever the outcome, one knows one must live in and through the times, be they opportune or inopportune, timely or untimely. One has no option but to chance one's luck and skill through troubled, disturbing, or exciting times.

A chance timing is an eruption in time beyond one's control and usually one's expectations. Its eventuality cannot be ignored; once materialised, chance acquires the qualities of necessity – it cannot be undone. In this sense, if only in this sense, time is irreversible; and chance becomes determining in its effects. There can never be a time for chance. It occurs, each time, sui generis: beyond calculation, and for the moment inexplicable. There is, however, always time for chance. And thus its grip, its lure, its agonising magnetism to those with something at stake. Will it strike? Can one continue for just one more month, week, day – undisturbed, as it were – or are one's hopes, rewards, career, one's entire life's goal to be dashed, at the' – last moment, by some chance event: some particular chance event, which at any other time could likely be accommodated, even ignored; but not now, not at this moment. The timing could not be worse. Its announcement could not be more untimely.

We need to stress this extreme chanciness inherent in timing, in *political time*. What is involved is not merely knowing why an event occurs. This may be discovered, even if only subsequently, and it is the privileged arena of our many scholarly disciplines. Such a thing was liable to happen, it can be concluded. But why it occurred exactly then is the question our human and physical sciences hardly answer. At best they may talk of probabilities and of the equal possibility that 'it' occurred then as much as at certain other times. If we still refused to acknowledge chance, we would soon be in the realm of either 'superstition' or 'paranoia', or into that which Roland Barthes referred to as a science of the particular, a 'mathesis singularis'. But timing involves more chance even than this, because what is at stake is nothing less than the coincidence of that particular event with an indeterminable number of other events or situations. Timing is a relationship, rather innumerable relationships, the complete knowledge of which by any point of inquiry is inconceivable. Some particular tragedy coming on the very eve of one's departure is, for example, outside the interest and information of most others unaffected by either event.

For those people actively and constantly engaged in promoting and engineering their own fortunes (one immediately thinks of the worlds of politics and finance as paradigm arenas) a heightened consciousness towards chance can be assumed. Some people intuitively know, for example, that chance can always open up a chance, an opportunity – or can kill it. Such people, we may imagine, are always ready for chance, at least psychologically. They are less shocked than others by an untimely blow or by, alternatively, the most timely of visitations. Despite their own many skills, training and apparent autonomy they may very well be true believers in social and personal fortuitousness. Theory, design, experience, science, they realise, can go only so far: after that it is nothing but chance. The newspaper reads: 'Having reached the deputyleadership, it must have looked [to X] that nothing but time stood between him and the premiership. But...'. Another time interfered with that time. The intended uneventful space, the calm period of doing nothing 'to rock the boat' suddenly counted for nothing. In these circumstances one has little option but to retire from that game, to re-plan one's future, to imagine new scenarios with their different set of times, their different circumstances and their different necessities. A new schedule, a new timetable, has to be calculated.

To others, the timing of an adventitious event may be quite traumatic. (have we two psychological types here: the one unflappable, the other on-edge no matter what the occasion?). Many people simply assume an orderly process in their personal or communal life history. They know, as it were, the assured temporal sequence of events. Whether linear or cyclical, time's future unfolding holds no doubts for them. A disruption, at any time, to such a view of things, is beyond normal speculation; and is, one imagines, beyond normal credulity and tolerance. An untimely, unexpected and unwelcome event can destroy. At the least it can generate doubt, uncertainty, anxiety and panic. Ultimately it can foster arbitrary, hasty, contradictory and unproductive and uncharacteristic behaviour. It can destroy one's basic trust in the future, in planning and calculation, in the very idea of a predictable life.

So, in *political time*, we plan the 'unplannable'. But we have no option. Whether we have been made wise by experience and inclination or whether we remain innocent or gullibly optimistic we are forced time and again to act according to the whims of chance, to changing times, to untimely tests of our strengths, flexibilities and qualities of adjustment. Do we fall victim, or become master, of time's fortunes? *Political time* brings out all these demands, and tests us. Together, timeliness and untimeliness open gateways, erect barriers, dictate scenarios, and significantly shape the distribution of rewards and punishments.

This mode of time, this timing, is not neutral; it has value. It is loaded, abundant, powerful. It is of such a potential and potent force that it is like some absolute power: absolute not merely in its degree, but in its supreme position, like a power of powers, like a god that can as readily cast you down as lift you up on high. It is not by chance that the Greeks had *Kairos* (the opportune time for action) as well as *Kronos* (sequential time) among their gods.

It is not a simple matter of time passing, of it improving or worsening a situation, of some gradual evolution. It is not simply that things may get better – or worse. Timing makes every moment potentially precarious; there is no guarantee at all that one's position at a moment of time will be the same, or similar, in the next moment of time. It is master. In terms of timing, time remains always in control. This is something that neither modern science nor a modernist culture can even begin to bring under its sway. Time orders the day; and in a way, by the sheer randomness of its apparent willful fallings, it produces a component of disorder into whatever systematic continuity and predictability humans have managed to engineer. Timing is the great destroyer of systems, of calculation, of a smooth life and history.

But time is not only something to dread. Because of it, and only because of it and its unpredictability, can there be hope. Hope is no carefully calculated and measured prediction; it is nothing more than a belief, and one not easily shaken, that, irrespective of appropriate signs, time may suddenly turn one's fortune. Times, it is known, do change. Timing is powerful: at one extreme it may halt and arrest hu-

man affairs in the most decisive manner of any inter-
dictory power; at the other it may permit or provide
the opportunity and means to achieve something in
the most accommodating of enabling power. Time
remains in control; despite all the ways by which time
has been unified, segmented, recorded and desacral-
ised by modern man, the timing of time remains outside any human mastery.

Timing is contextualising. It entails a location, or
rather a locating, in time and space – in an exception-
ally emphatic way. Timing cannot be universalised,
made eternal or absolute; to the degree that it has
an essence, it involves the idiosyncratic, the individual
instance, the unique moment, the never quite repeat-
able event. It is, in this sense, to be distinguished from
what could be called seasonal time and astrological
time because they are characterised by pattern and
iterability more than most things are; indeed, repetition and a notion of fixed times to which one returns
in large part constitute their distinctive quality.

But timing is no simple location in time. We are
not concerned merely to place it in some sequential
order of events or, indeed, to explain by its context
how it got there, nor, even, to elaborate some simultaneity. Timing is neither quite a diachronic nor syn-
chronic study. Its relation to its context is of a more
intervening, explosive, nature. Timing is that point of
intersection, the cross-trajectory, of time and action.
It therefore belongs simultaneously and necessarily
to two axes. Being timely, or untimely, is thus neither

merely a question of time nor simply a matter of substance. If it were the latter, then we would need to be concerned solely with the universal, absolute value of each and every action in their timeless and space-less purity. We would be dealing with notions of the 'proper'. If it were the former, we could simply conjugate a grammar of temporality and assign fixed values to each and every time: this moment, for example, must be auspicious; that moment inauspicious. But it is both (or neither); by itself neither one nor the other axis can be sufficient. This creates complications, constraints, even paradoxes.

Timing is, of necessity, a study of relationships; to be precise, of two sets of relationships: first, that between an event and all existing situations, expectations and other coexisting episodes. Together they constitute a matrix of forces, the concern being what effect that event is going to have. Second, that between the time of its occurrence and the time of the other factors; that an event occurred, for example, immediately before or during another episode, has significance. Consider, for example, the heightened sensitivity to, and power of, the slightest unusual event during an election campaign. No wonder candidates count the minutes during such vulnerable days.

The relationships are elusive in more than one way. It seems difficult, if not impossible, to consider the substantive nature of the event, or those matters it may have an impact on, without sliding from this type of consideration to thinking of them as temporal operators; that is, to calculate the likely effects of timing as such. *When* something occurred, that is, its timing in relation to other timings, becomes as much an agent as the very quality of the event. Time moves in more than one sense of that word; it is not a passive container within which the real world passes and acts. Timing, therefore, entails a slippage back and forth between two forms of identity; but as neither seems complete without the other no identity ever comes to rest. There is a constant displacement operating. Paradoxically, despite timing being essentially about location, it nevertheless escapes all precise definition as it is beyond and between any location – in time or space.

This calculus of forces generates an additional set of relational problems. It concerns the boundaries of the event's impact, of discerning its context, because in no way is this an assured given. Nor can it be obviously and simply devised as if one were measuring the distance of impact of an earth tremor, that answer being an unproblematic question of lineal space from an epicentre. The timing of an event creates varying centres and degrees of impact according to each and every contextual element. One cannot determine distance, and hence relative vulnerabilities and immunities, until after the impact is felt. What may have been considered remote may show itself to be alarmingly close. Any simple spatial imagery misrepresents the nature of the relation. And once again we can note an operation of displacement: force is transferred from some event or situation to others — without, it would seem, any necessary dissipation of energy as it moves. In fact, we know only too well that such displaced forces are capable of being more powerful than an initial event. A remote assassination of an archduke, at a particular time, produced a protracted European-wide battleground. Contexts are malleable and unpredictable.

Those more adept at gauging likely contextual parameters are the better equipped to cope with the changing circumstances when they arrive. They are equipped to initiate responses on their own behalf. Awareness of timing and its likely repercussions is one distinguishing feature of successful or unsuccessful social actors: some 'miss the opportunity', 'let the chance go', or 'never saw it coming'; others 'saw the opening', 'never let an opportunity pass', are 'always on the lookout', and 'ready for the main chance'. Through an agility and flexibility of response, an apparently insignificant or irrelevant event can be used, turned to someone's significant advantage. An unfortunate twist of affairs can be 'met half-way', and to some degree averted, redefined, rechanneled, even recouped. Because of its time and place, and because of the unimaginative response, it may, however, wreak disaster.

Timing eludes most of our conventional modes of classification. It is neither a simple matter of substance nor a mere question of time. While neither quality can ever be ignored we can never be satisfied with any one formulation. Timing eludes us in any of our efforts at determinate knowledge – and yet it remains so apparent, so real, so powerful. Whenever we feel we have captured it, pinned it down, it slides away. It is never just here or there. It is never present; it is always somewhere else.

It also eludes the conventional classification of being either objective or subjective; it so obviously breaches this simple choice. It is both. Consider a simple retirement from public office. It would appear a straightforward objective fact – but only if one considers it in isolation, outside its time and place. In its context it becomes a golden opportunity for some, with either a marginal adjustment, or an accelerated process of moves, or a radical redefinition of a career path. To others, it may destroy long-nurtured plans simply by coming when it did, or it may hint at a potential opening elsewhere. It may end a friendship, begin a new alliance. It cannot be divorced from its innumerable and particular subtexts in which it is interpreted, re-described, responded to, ignored. Its emergence is not singular. An event is a multiple fountainhead, a complex of signs diagnosed variously and located in a web of social scenarios and psychological matrices. It is subjected to human variations. It is at no stage one thing; it is a series of differences of an un-definable collection of social actors suddenly catapulted into participation in one or another of many exercises each of which has a life history and timespan of its own.

But it is certainly not something merely subjective, a matter of free-play and unrestrained idiosyncratic speculation. Anything does not go. No matter how wide and bizarre the range of imaginative responses may be, there are limits imposed by certain incontrovertible features of the original event or timing, limits that can never be confidently enumerated. However simple the event, it seems impossible to imagine all conceivable descriptions, receptions and responses. If a timing constructs a system it is one whose boundaries are un-definable.

Timing also defeats the simple distinction between passive and active. As we have seen, time itself seems to acquire all the trappings of any social agency; it happens, it acts, it causes. And yet, as if warned against inclinations to reify, we immediately draw back from this language, and concede that time is, in fact, acted upon, used, manipulated, is the passive object – perhaps merely a convenient figure of speech rather than any active agent. Even that re-description fails to satisfy: timing is not a thing that may be active or passive, it exists only in its relationships with other moments, timings and durations, and considered in this light it is perhaps best seen as beyond such distinctions of mood, or between them. But do we not need to go even further? Timing, in a way, is not a thing, not a concept, not anything conceivable. Timing, ultimately, is that which makes possibilities possible. Not an event, not a time, it allows the making of events and times. It is that which creates form, permits, even compels, a shaping of social reality. Timing is the seed which generates the very contours and passions of social action; without it there would be none – not unlike Jorge Luis Borges's attempt to capture the paradox of time.

> Time is the substance I am made of. Time is a river which sweeps me along, but I am the river; it is a tiger which destroys me, but I am the tiger; it is a fire which consumes me, but I am the fire (Borges 1964: 234).

Timing, as a specific moment in time (and space) is, at the same time, timeless. This quite specific moment has actually no precise beginning nor end in time or space, and again for the reason that it is a relationship. To be conceivable, timing must be related to times and timings which precede it and follow it. A location implies points of reference; without them it cannot be. Timing, therefore, always needs certain component parts of itself to pre-date it. It is in this sense always already there. A hypothetical retirement, for example, acquires a timing significance only because of other careers, ambitions, plans and prospects already afoot. It does not demand any particular time or relationship with its precedent parts for an event to have timing. Any time suffices. A timing is strategic to and for certain interests whenever it occurs. Timing emerges even when an apparently non-event like a decision not to retire occurs. A decision not to act, when a possibility of action is there, acquires all the qualities of any timing-event.

If we were to investigate when those preceding components began we would have to concede that, as has been argued persuasively in other contexts, there is no clear, unambiguous moment of origin. We certainly have no cause to assume a beginning from some latest, retrospective moment of consciously planned change. Intention has only a limited credibility here as elsewhere; its strategic value compared with forces beyond our conscious awareness is lean. And each moment of a life or history bears traces of earlier and then again earlier moments. If, for expedience, we were to limit an analysis to things close at hand, in time and space, we must not thereby assume that this conceptually exhausts the past. We could, perhaps, strategically decide that reference to current affairs and recent history were to be read as condensed signs of unstated (and often unknown) distant history. Once again, this suggested timelessness of the timely ought to remind us how misleading our spatial metaphors of distance and proximity are in interpreting human affairs. Furthermore, response to an event may, actually, be yet again some 'repetition compulsion', a response to an ancient experience, long forgotten or repressed. Our past is before us (in that useful ambiguity) as much as it is anywhere. The future of a timely event likewise stretches beyond time. Only in terms of our normal conscious span of curiosity do we end the study of effects after the first or second round of responses – as if the 'aftermath' of an event ended with the 'second mowing' of a season! The timing of an event is ultimately beyond our ideas of time and space. It is as much everywhere as nowhere in particular.

Such arbitrariness and elusiveness of beginnings, however, serve as a useful reminder that social response is necessarily a matter of *bricolage*, as Claude Lévi-Strauss expressed it: we have 'always to make do with 'whatever is at hand'. He used it to describe the behaviour of 'savages', as distinct from modern man, in the era of 'engineering technology' (Lévi-Strauss 1962). I am inclined to agree with Jacques Derrida, who argues that it applies to everyone. We are always, in one way or another, 'caught on the hop' by time (Derrida 1967). Things do not proceed, undisturbed, to some natural point of fruition, after which we carefully conceive and engineer anew our next grand venture: interrupted play in the norm. Unfinished business, some process abruptly disrupted, displaced or even destroyed by an event's occurrence – this is the reality of uneven change. Under such circumstances we can do little more than 'ad lib', reassess the new situation, calculate new plans, envisage new goals, and make an adjustment, welcome or otherwise, to our life's story. It is never the time, and there is no time, for the careful creation of appropriate and original technologies. Somehow or other we put together the next project out of the contingent parts of a past and future. Somewhat ironically, we are determined, in large part, by the chance timings which befall us, and by the contingencies which follow.

We could say that the result can never be more than a timely compromise. To begin, it is, of necessity, a mediation with time as any step will have to be on time. There are no spatio-temporal interregna allowing us to regroup at leisure and to recommence whole. In a most complex way, all history, personal or collective, is necessarily uneven, heterogeneous, partial, out of step and, in that sense, constantly discontinuous irrespective of continuities possible at some other level of understanding. Some timing or other is constantly erupting on the social or individual scene. We regroup as best we can, we retime (reset) our scenarios, attempt to adapt, pragmatically, never able to start afresh from first principles. And the many different times we find ourselves engaged in at any one time can never be neatly coordinated. We are one step behind and one step ahead. We never occupy the same space or time. In a way, there is no same space and time there for us, potentially, to occupy. Our judicious notions of fit, evenness, and coordination are thrown into disarray.

We understandably assume that our language (for example, in this case English) provides us with everything we need to describe the various qualities of timing: I refer here, specifically, to the words 'timely' and 'untimely', the one indicating notions of good or satisfactory timing, the other its opposite. But these words are not as accommodating as they appear; they contain a hidden agenda, traces of their past, as well as the hopes and fears of generations of language users. We are, in fact, constrained from saying what we may want to say about timeliness, but we are unaware of this; it has been effectively repressed. The language has been crafted to fit our deepest desires.

Middle English usage of these words was tied to nature whose visitations were taken as predictable. Seasons were definable, unambiguous and, in primary economies of farming and fishing, all determining. Essentially referring to the weather, to be timely meant 'appearing in good time, early, seasonal'; to be untimely meant 'coming before the proper or natural time, premature, unseasonable in respect of time of year' (*Shorter Oxford Dictionary*). This usage is confirmed by the main synonym of timely – opportune – acquired early from the French and referring to the prevailing nature and direction of the wind, and specifically meaning 'drawing towards the harbour, hence seasonable' – thus ensuring the safe return to 'port' of the fishing fleet.

This early usage of the language of timing is over-determined. Words were made to fit a notion of a proper order of things. To be timely referred not only to that which is appropriate seasonally, but to that which is, accordingly, predictable and expected (spring weather in spring, winter weather in winter) and, finally, to that which best suits the needs of the people, always constructed as congruent with the weather. Rain, or sunshine, for example, is expected and needed at one time and not another. The very notion of timeliness had a tidy, simple and efficient dual economy about it. Being timely, the dominant part of the hierarchical pair, referred to that coincidence of time, event, need and expectation which was wholly desirable; untimely being the aberration or lack of fit – a particular (bad) weather condition arriving at the wrong time, thus not expected and, necessarily, having an undesirable effect. Not unlike the ungodly, the untimely was, if possible, to be avoided; but, of course, it lay beyond human volition.

What is of interest is the symmetry and fullness of the linguistic schema; it satisfied all the needs at the time. It covered adequately all contingencies, which in fact were, conceptually, only two: what was desirable and what was undesirable conditions. Timeliness, tied to the seasons, *prohibited* certain considerations: it was meaningless, and so impossible to think, for example, of an unexpected occurrence which could be good, or of something predictable which could be bad. 'Being on time' or 'not being on time' said everything. They were condensed linguistic symbols representing time, event, expectation and consequence. No event was of an absolute, universal or objective value; everything was contextual, but in that special sense of fixed, proper and total context, of an ideal, congruent fit.

Modern usage is untied from nature and its seasonal character. To be timely now means being 'well-timed, opportune'; to be untimely 'ill-timed, inopportune', and so we imagine a good or bad timing can now occur at any time. That is, the previous connection with expectations is severed; we can now, for the first time, conceptualise and experience equally a 'timely surprise' or an 'untimely surprise', the former previously unthinkable. We, perhaps, could expect comparable flexibility regarding the timing of any kind of event: that is, again loosened from seasonally determined activities, a welcome event and an unwelcome event may occur at any time. But, interestingly, we are not equipped in language to handle such flexible situations and judgments. The words timely and untimely have, without our awareness, maintained a trace of their past. For some event to be considered timely, it *still* needs to be a pleasurable event: we cannot refer to a 'timely disaster' without appearing selfcontradictory or perverse. It would be seen as an oxymoron; a disaster apparently does not 'go' with, does not fit, *any* idea of timeliness. Obviously, we suddenly realise – there is no suitable or appropriate time for painful events; our unconscious psyche not our rational logic has ensured that our language reflects this. By fiat, a disaster must always be seen as untimely. However, it can happen that sometimes a delayed consequence (a deferred time) of a disastrous event is, surprisingly, welcome. It may, for example, force us to do something beneficial which we otherwise would not have done; we needed that painful stimulus, apparently, to act. Then, in retrospect, we may reflect on the irony and conclude that 'the disaster was, perhaps, after all, timely'. The event is revalued and re-signed as a timely warning. A mirror-image of this asymmetry can be seen with the contradiction of an 'untimely reward': there is no time that pleasure is not welcome; a reward is always timely. However, once again, we may look back with wisdom and note, ironically, how some apparent reward later turned sour making the celebrations of the time premature, untimely. If we had only known at the time!

So, notions of timeliness are flexible but normally more geared to the nature of the event – as it is defined at any time; desirable ones being prima facie timely, undesirable ones untimely. Matters of degree provide the only difference: certain times may be more or less timely (or untimely) than others. It also remains a matter of taste for irony whether a timely reward is most welcome when everything is going well or when everything is going badly. Similarly, it is a matter of taste, and temporal distance, whether misfortune is better to occur at the height or nadir of one's fortune.

The calculation and judgment of an event were properly and simply coordinated in earlier times, and constituted and manifested a condensed sign. One could know. Such an over-determined fit and certainty of judgment seem no longer available to us. But then, perhaps, we may demand more of the language these days.

And maybe the most powerful and most pervasive demand on our time is that of chance, which previously may have conceptually played less significant a role. These days, it seems, anything can happen at any time, with any consequence. This is not to say that chance events occur more frequently now than they did (although spatio-temporal communications make us more sensitive, responsive and vulnerable today to a range of global chances). Rather we are now more dependent on things not patterned by seasonal and tidal forces. Are we perhaps aware of the general chanciness which surrounds us and within which we must plot our course? Events overwhelm; they press and ramify: we are constantly mollified or harassed by the timing of things. No segment of our life is uneventful.

The demise of ideas of the 'proper' (a word and notion that has had a powerful impact on the West), in one form or other, seems characteristic of western modernity. While properness still manifests itself in so many ways, there does appear to be, nevertheless, a significant pervasive loss of faith in a natural order of things which somehow determines how and what things go, or ought to go, together: a mode of ontological disenchantment. To the degree that this is so, one wonders what role has been played here by a sensing (rather than a 'dis-consciousness') that 'time is out of kilter', that there is no proper order in time, that things occur in disarray rather than in harmony with another; that, in plotting our lives, we are constantly obliged to change plans; that, because of the varied timeliness of change, the oddest things are bed-fellows; that the strange coexist, rather than the similar remaining canonically placed together. The timing of things helps to ensure that social reality appears more a disparate collage – stuck, glued, pasted together – than a system whose congruent, wedded parts naturally cohere. ('Collage' in colloquial French refers to a man and woman living together without being married; an unnatural, that is, im-proper, coupling; 'living-in-sin', as it has been labeled by some!)

It is also sometimes wondered whether irony is the trope most appropriate and representative of the 20th Century. I wonder whether these two putative trends could be related and whether they find their bond in a common attitude to timeliness? The *Shorter Oxford Dictionary* reminds us that the sense of irony is 'a contradictory outcome of events as mockery of the promise and fitness of things'. What a telling description of the vagaries of timing we have been discussing! No matter how often and carefully we read the signs to confirm some promise of things, no matter how much we secretly believe in, or hope for, the fitness of things, times prove us wrong; what we are not expecting, let alone want, often eventuates. And it is both the most opportune and the inopportune turn of events which equally demand our attention, test resources and compel adjustment to the state of affairs. Whether we fully appreciate it or not, time after time portrays an ironic outcome: 'And then that happened!', 'That that should have occurred then!' Time dissembles and mocks. Even as we look, yet another twist occurs. Once more we have been deceived, tricked, misled; expecting one thing, we are delivered another. This is ironic enough at any time of history, but surely especially ironic in the 20th-century western world which, for at least three hundred years, has culturally denied a role to chance, are allowed to say is an expression of our hidden and simple wishes and fantasies. The irony is surely both timely and untimely.

Is there a final irony? If western man (it is only western man who has nurtured a faith in his own potential omnipotence; western woman has not had the opportunity to become so deluded) were to concede that time dictates to him more than he to it, how would he then distinguish himself from those 'superstitious' people elsewhere whose faith in their own potency was always tempered by a respect towards more impersonal and remote forces? Would such a reorientation constitute a step towards or beyond Enlightenment?

I began by referring to timing as a study of *political time*. I did so for certain political reasons, a move I now need to re-consider.

The study of politics has been too much determined by a tradition which informs us that the punitive and coercive concepts of power and authority are its unquestionably central and identifying characteristics. And, as Michel Foucault pointed out, this is normally interpreted to mean that politics is an activity in which there are those (a minority) with power or authority and others (the majority) without. Whether conscious or not, a hierarchical or juridical model has been, and still is, the accepted mode of analysis. Despite certain efforts, it is still uncommon for political power to be treated in a relational manner in which initiatives or responses (assuming for the moment they can be separated) are not firmly and inherently embedded in particular hierarchical socio-spaces. The analysis of political issues is ultimately settled by recourse to a mechanical zero-sum calculation, a difference in quantity only, a recourse to a homogenized space whose proportional shares are both measurable and divisible, and, as it were, answerable.

The study of politics has been too much determined by a tradition which informs us that the punitive and coercive concepts of power and authority are its unquestionably central and identifying characteristics. And, as Michel Foucault pointed out, this is normally interpreted to mean that politics is an activity in which there are those (a minority) with power or authority and others (the majority) without. Whether conscious or not, a hierarchical or juridical model has been, and still is, the accepted mode of analysis. Despite certain efforts, it is still uncommon for political power to be treated in a relational manner in which initiatives or responses (assuming for the moment they can be separated) are not firmly and inherently embedded in particular hierarchical socio-spaces. The analysis of political issues is ultimately settled by recourse to a mechanical zero-sum calculation, a difference in quantity only, a recourse to a homogenised space whose proportional shares are both measurable and divisible, and, as it were, answerable.

On the other hand, we are surely all conscious of the way certain commentators, politicians and a particular sophisticated public refer to the preferred, if not essential quality of political behaviour as realistic or pragmatic. This means implying, invariably, that while politicians would prefer, of course, to do something else, the given circumstances (times) oblige them both to (temporarily) relinquish such ideal goals, and to pursue more timely ones – which after a while tend to be presented as if they were the ideal goals. Confronting such apologists are others who define such behaviour as 'opportunist', as too ready to sell out on higher principles for the expedience of the moment. Depending on the audience, therefore, the same word, pragmatist, can be considered laudatory or derogatory; the same action can be labeled affirmatively as realistic, or negatively as opportunist

It seems politically important, now, to engage with this issue – one in which time and timing are central concerns of this apparent paradox receive scant attention from most students of politics. I also want to suggest that there are many properties related to timing – the necessary, urgent bricolage of action; behaviour as an unclear mixture of initiative and blind, hasty grabbing whatever is at hand; a strategic play of chance and necessity; the unevenness of social reality. We can add the drama, surprise, tension, and the essentially psychological element in action; and the centrality rather than marginality of unintended consequences. In a much enlarged sense, these are together perhaps more significant as inherent qualities of politics than limited, conventional notions of power and authority. Having said that, however, we must acknowledge immediately that politics, as this complex operation, exists in fields other than the political as narrowly conceived. Politics is ubiquitous. Such a declaration could reduce human action to so many expressions of some basic drive for power, or knowledge, or reason, for good or bad. It expands their subjectivity and it recognises that in whatever position they find themselves they are both determined and determining; that they can never hope to escape the pincers of time; that each moment of life creates a play between the restraints and opportunities jointly offered by time.

I say time. Having proposed that *political time* ought to be seen in its most pervasive and catholic garb of timing rather than in some narrow sectarian cloth of official politics, I now want to propose that we replace the concept of time by timing. Could we suggest, tentatively, that timing is, in one way, a most tangible quality of time; that time occurs only as timing, as something in no way transcendental, universal, absolute, even and beyond history, but always as something dressed with and by an event. It emanates a particular and elusive quality; it has always the touch of some historical moment about it but, at the time, its temporality is inescapably ineffable;

timing is neither precisely here nor there, it is always elsewhere. It is the essential displacement, a timeless chimera.

Politics, as life itself, is the fluctuatingly enviable and unenviable play of the opportune and the inopportune; of the timeliness and untimeliness of all that occurs in reality; of the constant intercourse of chance and necessity; of how we can, or could, handle our circumstances; of how our contexts can be as much an opening as a closure, an excuse, a challenge. Timing is our entire history in the fullness of that term; it regulates and deregulates our every activity.

It seems now time to draw back and quickly to rewrite historical time. We have seen how the most chancy event determines the moves which follow, shutting out certain consequences and highlighting others as likely responses: the decline of contingency, the rise of necessity. Yet, if this is so, surely we must concede that the event itself is likely to be in some way just another determined consequence of yet one further, past event. And so back and back in time. At the very moment we are ready to surrender ourselves as mere pawns of chance we can, at once, rethink ourselves as pawns of complex determinisms. The degree of play from chance to necessity suddenly appears surprisingly small after all.

A move from chance to determinism becomes even more plausible if we were now to adjust our idea of 'event'. There is no reason to restrict such timed occurrences to the momentary affairs we have up till now mentioned. There is no conceptual need to place any time limit on events: a ten-year war, a two-hundred-year colonial rule, a post-Enlightenment epoch, the Christian era – nothing about their genesis, function and impact distinguishes them from instantaneous times like births, deaths and resignations. And with this change of perspective we appreciate more the pattern of things, and we realise that it is not by accident that certain things at times are more liable to occur here than there, now than then, and we once again sense that science and the search for knowledge do have some role to play after all.

But this may be a new science: one attuned to the play of chance and necessity, to the centrality of timing and spacing, to the contextual nature of social reality as it engages its past and its future, to the relative powers of time and humans. Only then may we begin to know what, in some circumstance, was possible, what was beyond control, and for what one could be held responsible.

Comparative studies would require a radical redefinition; universal moral judgments arising from a timeless language and schema of thing would need to be eschewed; and a certain caution prized. We would also recognise that it will always be too early for final explanations: that what is timely at one time may well be untimely at another. It is all about time.

Chapter Six. The Gift of Timing

Beginnings and ends

Timing is there, at the beginning and at the end. Medical science, and long before that, folk knowledge, has known the importance of managing the moment of birth; which moment, exactly when. The significance of being right – of being right on time. Is the child in the womb 'ready'? To come too soon has its set of problems; to come too late another set. A 'natural' birth is well timed, finely tuned; it arrives just at the right moment. Minimal pain to the mother and child. Nature, it seems, knows and cares. Could we even say that nature naturally times a birth, and times it naturally? How artificial, 'unnatural', untimely is that which decides, for good or foolish reason, to determine the time of birth by other means. The 'caesarean' birth ('the delivery of a child by cutting through the walls of the abdomen' as the Oxford dictionary describes it) may, from some perspective be seen as well timed; it obviously suits someone's timetable. From another it is surely seen as necessarily most untimely. The very violence of the act is there in the dictionary definition of the cut. At the least it is a birth which ostensibly ignores questions of timing, deciding to slash away at some moment of convenience, or danger. We begin through such a choice. A timely entry into the world, an easing into a social existence, may augur well, one imagines, for body and spirit.

And we end, once again either well or poorly timed. Is there an ideal time? We regret the passing of those persons, even strangers we merely read about, dying far too early: in the prime of their lives, in their youth, in their infancy. It seems unfair, a waste of a life, a waste of time, pointless, cruel. But, if that is considered far too soon, we nevertheless complain, yet perhaps not as resolutely, when life seems to stretch on and on, beyond its time. Death could be a timely visitation, albeit late. To end it all. Is there a time to die? Can we live too long? Can we sense or learn to tell the right time? Time to go. Finished, rounded everything off, completed all the tasks, made farewells. To linger on after this is in some way offensive, redundant, a lack of taste, or at least a lack of consideration for others. We have a duty to others, it would seem, even as we calculate ourselves. We must not over-stay our life. 'But I thought he had died a long time ago! What has he been doing lately? Who?' – all express an embarrassing untimeliness. Each life, it seems, has its appropriate length. We have an ideal image what it is, no matter how poorly articulated it may be – and no matter how this may vary across cultures.

Perhaps our death begins at birth? Life is little more, from one perspective, than a preparation for death. It is not only Freud who has sensed a vital (sic!) relationship between beginnings and ends. 'The goal of all life is death', he dramatically announced in *Beyond the Pleasure Principle* (Freud 1922). There is an urge inherent in organic life to restore an earlier state of things (but) the organism wishes to die only in its own fashion. As Peter Brooks elaborates, if the repetition compulsion and the death instinct serve the pleasure principle, in a larger sense, the pleasure principle serves the death instinct, making sure that the organism is permitted to return to quiescence: 'The organism must live in order to die in the proper manner, to die the right death. We must have the 'arabesque' of plot in order to reach the end' (Brooks 1977). To die the right death is a well-timed journey which ends at the appropriate moment. A time for everything. And, strictly speaking, never too much time.

Foucault spells out, in his archaeology of medical perception, Birth of the Clinic, a remarkably similar dynamic dependency of life and death in which we can sense the two paradoxically timing each other in a fanciful intertwining of 'cause' and 'effect'. Since the early nineteenth century, he tells us, we realise that:

> death is that against which life in daily practice, comes up against; in it the living being resolves itself naturally: and disease loses its old status as an accident, and takes on the internal, constant, mobile di-

mension of the relation between life and death. It is not because he falls ill that man dies; fundamentally, it is because he may die that man may fall ill. And beneath the chronological life/disease/death relation, another, earlier, deeper figure is traced: that which links life and death, and so frees, besides, the signs of disease (Foucault 1963).

Are our familiar signs of life signs of death? Instead? As well? Can we tell the time any more, even though every moment now appears to be timed?

'It is only a question of time' conjures up anxiety. Pressure. Running out of time. It depends. 'Astronomers in Britain issued a warning in April 1992 that the Earth would be hit by an asteroid with the destructive force of a million H-bombs. The possibility of a collision is far greater than has been realised, one astronomer is reported in the press as saying: 'We expect these things to hit us. It is only a question of time'. The fainthearted can rest assured, the report continues. It is unlikely to happen for a few hundred thousand years' (*The Age*, April 10, 1992). It is primed; determined. It may or may not be on time when it comes. But it's on target. It can be counted on.

Timing and tennis – and beyond

Again, timing is fundamental to tennis, as it is most likely to all games, from cricket and golf to chess. There are two aspects to it – a micro and a macro element – we'll see how these expressions have limited use only. Micro-timing is more basic it seems – meaning it is based on physical motor co-ordinations – perceptions, seeing the ball well, speed of bodily movement, the change in body weight. Everyone has some timing for without it one could not even hit the ball. Excellent timing is rare. With quality, one can hit the ball sooner, for example on half-volley, which reduces the time for the opponent to prepare and hit, that is, one is thereby in a position to apply increased pressure on the opponent – to try to upset his timing, to rattle him; one can use the speed of the delivery to your advantage thus expending less of your own force. In some strange way, your power is your opponent's power. This 'dependent relationship' symbolises the lack of any precise, definite boundary between the play (strokes etc.,) of the two players. One's stroke is never solely yours. Thus, statistics of forced and unforced errors is based on a very dubious distinction.

This talent cannot be taught – it is intuitive. Training can improve anyone – within degrees. Very much like a talent for metaphor as Aristotle said: 'a sign of genius' (*Poetics*, 1459a 5-8). The word 'timing' thus used in two senses; that which is necessary to begin playing a game (species); and the exceptional ability, as if Timing with capital letter: John McEnroe has Timing. Thus, a television commentator can say: 'he didn't really strike the ball, just timed it perfectly'.

Touch is and is not the same as ideal timing: for example, executing certain drop-shots demands a unique control. A nuance, a subtlety, a grace, a deli-

cacy, a gentleness, an elegance. This distinguishes the
best from the rest – the former is an artist. An interesting use of that word. I am sure all commentators
would use it accordingly; in sport, even in a violent
contact sport like football, the player with timing and
touch would be referred to as an 'artist'. Why? It is
more than a matter of style, surely! But then, how
broad do we want to make style? If it is art, is it just
one characteristic art?, that is, one with panache, flair,
talent? So, is timing (in this micro sense) a talent? We
need to know more before we could say if it is 'only
talent', that is, something else crucial is missing.

Which brings us to the second, macro meaning
of timing – the strategic sense. This is more cerebral
(cognitive?) than the first's physical, perceptual, bodily character. Here, it is an appreciation of the match/
encounter in its entirety – quite distinct from a plan of
play – though that may well be a part of it. Such play
knows one can lose a battle without necessarily losing
the war. Borg was master in using the entire five sets.
He worked himself into the game, even if this meant
he lost the first two sets. He was not thrown by this.
So, in a sense, it is timing, this time, as the psychology
of the game. It makes distinctions between different
parts. All is not the same, each game is not equal to
all others. Again, this psychology must not be seen as
something merely 'subjective' – as if divorced from
the real actuality of the game. It is, rather, the psychological appreciation of each stage of the match,
or each game, for what it is (either as very impor-

tant or all the way to relative expendability). Is it a question of relative costs? To serve a double-fault on match-point is fatal; to serve one while 40/00 up is not. It entails not freezing up on crucial points, that is, during a tie-break. In that sense it means treating all points equally. But that is clearly inadequate. It surely means appreciating the relative worth of each stage or point and playing them all appropriately. Is this the key word? If so, what does it mean? It is the timeliness of the particular shot attempted; which means that a reckless, high-risk shot is timely or appropriate when one has a clear lead – a bonus if it works; if it fails it does not matter; whereas a greater element of care in an otherwise powerful shot is 'called for' (an interesting term) when the situation is more critically dangerous. Here we could say that certain imperatives ought to apply: one should not double-fault in a tie-break.

Perhaps a few imperatives, almost rules of good play, exist. More often, however, these may be more like rules of thumb to be applied with flexibility. Both, of course, imply there is one clear goal – to win (this becomes relevant as we will see). Timeliness or appropriateness also should suggest that changing-ness rather than a fixed program of play should operate. That is, as the game proceeds, a variety of factors will change the fortunes of the players: one moment secure, the next in trouble. One's play, one's appropriate play is a response of these changing fortunes – again the strategy of timing is a product of the relationship between the players; each moment of the game tells a new 'truth' of the match; one cannot therefore predict with any degree of certainty what one should be doing next game. Is there a relationship between the two senses of timing, between the technique and the strategy? Perhaps there isn't. A military parallel can illustrate. An inferior army/force can win a war through superior strategy – for example, guerilla warfare.

Strategic timing, however, can be seen from perspectives broader than a single match. The two weeks of a competition implies that ideal timing is to attain one's peak at the end of the second week. A top player does not want to peak prematurely – that's poor timing. And even broader: the timing of the season or year of competition. It would be bad timing to peak at Queens rather than at Wimbledon, which immediately follows. One paces oneself during the year just as much during a match or a tournament. Like a long-distance race, marathon in particular. Different demands are appropriate at different stages of the race, yet always needing to remember the distance as a whole. The Australian track athlete Herb Elliott was skilled at timing himself in a race whereas his compatriot long-distance runner Ron Clarke was not – he could race against the clock but not against competitors.

Back to the relationship between the two timings. One may be good at one but not the other. French tennis player Henri Leconte's timing in hitting the ball was first class but his sense of match-time was totally missing. He played all points the same in a high-risk way. He could, psychologically, not play safe shots either when that was all that was required to win a point or when he was at a critical, even vital, moment of a game or set. He was too bold, irresponsible, cavalier – childish. All this can be explained in a different definition of the game. That is, he did not have only one goal – to win, and the strategic sense of timing assumes that. No, we can surely say that Leconte was interested in other achievements: to entertain himself and others, to enjoy himself, to thrill, to shock, even to set himself demanding mini-goals, for example, to win a point the impossible way. Caution he seemed to despise. All this made people like him enormously – but perhaps not admire him. Or did they secretly do that as well? (Australia's Evonne Goolagong may have been more secretly loved for other reasons?) That is, Leconte was dramatically, obviously, over-abundantly non-professional that he secretly reminded us that it was all a game and nothing more, and that we should not take it too seriously. Thus, Leconte could never behave like a McEnroe – that manner of court-performance would make no sense to him.

Play and responsibility

Is this a (if not 'the') difference between 'play' and 'structure' as Derrida (1967) says of Lévi-Strauss' thesis? McEnroe 'works' at the structure of the match and senses the appropriate timing at all times and constructs the match (looking for words other than 'play') appropriately. The professional. Leconte, an amateur, plays the game for the games' sake. Is this post-modernist tennis? Everything is a diversion, a detour; nothing is a linear segment of the match; each point is unique, unconnected – or, only loosely attached to some whole.

Could we think of some equivalent for business or politics? Political play; business play. Surely these activities can be seen in other than the normal (modernist) one of serial structure, linear, unidirectional, step after step; chronology and cause and effect. Could Robert Holmes a-Court be an example of a player; Kerry Packer as a professional, a structuralist, a literalist? Economists assume that man is economic man: John Sambell (a banker) lives by the adage, 'if it was easy to be rich, everyone would be'. Ignoring his point of inevitably having losers for all winners, he assumes (without question) that there can only be one aim, the goal – transcendental – which provides the entire rationale of the operation – and a goal everyone strives for – missing out only because of luck or bad judgment, poor rationality. He does not entertain the possibility of a player, of someone doing a Leconte, of an amateur. Is this 'speculation'? a la Holmes a-Court? Is this the difference between business and gambling? No, I am sure it is not.

And political play? Is this the over-principled 'poli'? – who ignores the times and timing and does whatever he thinks correct despite the inevitable outcome. A paradox. To ignore time in politics one immediately thinks of the over-proper: the ideologue, idealist, the foolish, the innocent, for example, perhaps the 1970s Whitlam era Labor Party rebel Jim Cairns (to admirers an idealist; to critics foolish, innocent). To ignore timing in sport one thinks of the under-proper, the flippant, the lover, the not-too-serious. And to ignore timing in business is irresponsible, or stupid. Although the expression 'to ignore' implies a constant concern, not a momentary lapse. That is, one can suffer a short loss of concentration − it is expected in a tennis match − without being labeled 'irresponsible'. Or one can make mistakes − miscalculate what is expected to happen, often enough, in all areas of endeavour. That is, one's sense of timing could be wrong at a particular moment − which may or may not be fatal. One may be called 'unfortunate' − given the benefit of the doubt − a sympathy vote. But certainly not if one tends to do this too often; that is, by one's behaviour (by acts, decisions) and the regular bad consequences of this, that one is not concentrating enough on the circumstances, or that one's judgment is just unsatisfactory, or that one is merely insensitive to questions of timing, the climate, the changing circumstances, and so on. One could be judged disinterested in the job; or distracted because of pre-occupations elsewhere (personal, family problems − a reluctant tolerance will usually be shown if some reasonable familial concern is seen as an explanation). On any of these three counts one would be considered unsatisfactory material for the role. A severe moral judgment indeed. One could be tolerated only if one had another compensating attribute: in politics, say charisma and hence an electoral following; in business, say lots of money, connections and influence; in tennis (or sport) huge ability and hence attractiveness because of the style and talent in play – an innocent and appealing spectator-charm.

However, if under-utilising timing, hopeless timing, is condemned, there is also some degree of balancing criticism if timing is over-utilised (a too perfect timing). Let me elaborate. One could be considered too ruthless: so concerned to win (money, votes, the game) that one tries too hard. One is considered too competitive (in sport especially) in a way that is a form of qualification, or a dismissal, or a foolish admiration. Too serious, too mean, a bit inhuman like a robot. In business, feared and disliked; no friends, again a bit inhuman; too successful, too ambitious, needing some balance, humanity. In politics, again a ruthless competitor or an unscrupulous opportunist concerned only with the timing and nothing else. The one who explains everything in terms of circumstances and the fluctuating needs of the moment; everything fluid, nothing fixed or principled – yes, unprincipled in politics, but not in business. In military matters it is legitimate to think only in terms of winning the battle: surgical timing may be everything. Nothing but praise follows.

So there are rules of the game (even though unarticulated) concerning the broad, varying but nevertheless tangible parameters of timing within which one may and will be expected to operate, and thereby be approved. Outside of this one will be criticised, even condemned. One needs to fine-tune one's timing; to time one's timing!! One can be too right as much as too wrong. Humanness is seen as a shade peccable (from 16th century theology; *'peccare'* (Italian) to sin. Hence 'impeccable' not liable to sin).

Timing and responsibility

Responsibility is not exhausted by the simple distinction we have just made: the professional versus the amateur; the one to whom timing is everything because winning is paramount and timing is its essential strategy; the other to whom timing is nothing – one plays for the pleasure of each moment. To the first, time has a variable quality, one moment opportune and dense, other moments inopportune, worthless, to be ignored. To the second, time is uniform, but in the special sense that the only time considered is the present and that is always equally, highly valuable.

We need to go further, otherwise we will have left politics solely to that kind of person who is generally seen to think only tactically: the pragmatist, realist, even opportunist; that is, the person who constantly calculates the time and acts according to the dictates of the time, and it would seem , little else. But responsibility can come with more than one time-table. The timing of responsibility is not an unproblematic formula; it remains one always open to interpretation.

We can begin with a study of the fall of Bob Hawke from his record breaking term of being Australia's Prime Minister, and central to this story is his (ex) colleague, Senator Graham Richardson, 'the Machiavelli of Australian politics' and the pivotal figure in both Labor's Federal leadership changes in the past decade. Richardson saw the opportunity to topple Hawke and replace him with Paul Keating soon after John Kerin, who had replaced Keating as Treasurer, failed to seize an opportunity. Kerin had announced a one percent cut in interest rates merely with a press announcement. As Peter Hartcher, *The Age* journalist, comments: 'In one of Kerin's many inexplicable miscalculations, he lost a perfect opportunity to trumpet good news, to stir some confidence into a recessed economy' (*The Age*, May 2, 1992). One month later, after an embarrassing stumbling speech to the press, Kerin is sacked by Hawke who, preferring to delay it a few weeks, is nevertheless successfully talked into an immediate sacking by some of his colleagues, including Richardson. Richardson immediately appreciated the situation. 'He decided it was time to finish Hawke off. The contest for the Lodge (the Prime Ministerial residence) had reopened, and Richardson was determined to win. 'Within two days of Kerin's sacking, Richardson believed he had the numbers to win a challenge within the party'. It was the dispatch of Kerin that killed Hawke. Until that moment, the Keating campaign for the ultimate prize had been suspended. Little did Hawke know that Keating had given himself 'a self-imposed timetable' of only several more weeks for success (any longer and he believed he would have had insufficient time – fifteen months at the most – to win the next election as a new Labor Prime Minister). After that time he had decided to withdraw from politics entirely.

This was Keating's last chance, and Richardson knew it had to be resolved quickly. If the struggle were to linger on over the Christmas break, all the impetus of the challenge would be dissipated. Speed and coordination were both necessary. With great enthusiasm and secrecy, Richardson set about organising the systematic isolation of the Prime Minister. He set out to deprive Hawke of the support of his innermost political allies, of his Cabinet, of his political friends, even of his long-standing friends in the business world. He wanted it to become clear to Hawke that he was desperately, 'friendlessly' finished. He succeeded in all these moves but Hawke still would not give in. Finally, a vote in the party room was taken. Richardson's bet of 56 votes for Keating to 51 for Hawke was exactly right. A new Australian Prime Minister had been chosen – within thirteen days of the removal of Kerin. If it is accepted, as it certainly was by most within the Party, that Hawke would not win the next election then, despite his remarkable three terms of office, it was responsible for party members to consider his replacement by some-

one who may win. On that premise, Richardson's behaviour acquires credibility; it can be explained as an
unsavoury necessity – which, to succeed, had to be
ruthless, fast and total. A 'Machiavelli' is not, surely,
an unreasonable label.

However, there is no need to accept a conventional line of thought that only some such mode of behaviour as Richardson's, in which one is highly sensitive to the exigencies of time and opportunities, is the
only responsible one in politics. Responsibility is not
exhausted by the temporal dimension of immediacy:
today, tomorrow, next year. The timing of responsibility is a varied act. Consider Helene Cixous's discussion, in 1991, of deserts and disasters:

> We can also let ourselves be haunted by the
> Sakharov couple ... They must have within them-
> selves that treasure of treasures, the inextinguisha-
> ble spark of faith. They must have faith to remain
> alone, a trinket of voice against eight hundred
> million deaf ears. These are people who decided
> to stay where there are no ears. Their faith is that
> some day, somewhere, there will be open ears. It
> is not necessarily for tomorrow but perhaps in two
> hundred years (Cixous 1991).

And Cixous wonders what may produce a spring in
such deserts. It may be childhood, she suggests:

> Those who keep their childhood already have
> a world behind them ... It can be the heritage of
> those who wander, like the Jews, or of those who

have behind them the Book of History and a very long story that made them cross time. Those who have five thousand years behind them say to themselves that perhaps, in another five thousand, there will be something else ... 'All poets are Jews' (Cixous 1991, citing Marina Tsvetaeva)

We could also mention criticisms of President George H. Bush for being 'cowardly and short sighted' in his immediate responses to the tragedy of the Los Angeles riots after the trial dismissal of the four police accused of brutality against Rodney King. Bush certainly timed, that is, targeted his public responses to the L.A. affair, with the forthcoming Presidential elections as dominant goal. An emphasis on law and order is invariably perfectly, and cautiously, appropriate for such a purpose. If a Presidential victory is considered a responsible goal, and surely it must be, then Bush's response was impeccably timed.

But there may, of course, be other goals which are more distant, more intangible in nature and more difficult to measure in terms of their achievement and even of the efficacy of policies in their pursuit. We need not plan and act within some limited time span, even within our own life span. There are futures which can also be either lost or won. If one were concerned, for example, to attempt to eradicate the entrenched causes of black alienation in America, the timing could not have been more appropriate than in the immediate aftermath of the Los Angeles riots. A time of catharsis; the ideal moment for the symbolic gesture. All of this quite independent, of course, of the eventual success or not of measures to be taken. The opportunity was seized by others to announce a radical restructuring of their lives. Two of Los Angeles' notorious rival 'colour-gangs' called a truce. Members said they wanted to end black-on-black killing (which had been going on since 1967-8) and to build a unified power base to seize power for their (black) community. One gang leader said the time had come for peace.

The same occasion can be used or not used as an opportunity for many different things. Even a tragedy can be used auspiciously. Likewise, of course, a situation can be grabbed for the narrowest and most ephemeral of purposes thereby losing the opportunity for a grander view. Timing is manifold.

We still need to consider the relation between the two timings. The actual occurrence of good timing (in the first sense) can vary. One may have a bad day, or a bad set. In such a situation one's strategic timing, although good, may still be inadequate for winning. In that sense, neither of the two is the more important. But, being good at either one does not seem to affect the other: skills are independently based, created, nurtured, and there is little to suggest a transfer between the two. So, an internal struggle is possible; trying to get the two elements in sync.

With either timing, we can distinguish an awareness from an accomplishment. We probably all know what one should do – to time the ball, to time the play. That does not guarantee that we will successfully execute them.

A connection at last: the ideal, ultimate in tennis: to time the union of the two timings. To bring it all together. In sync, of course. And this finally is beyond us: we can prepare – practice both things in theory and actuality as much as possible – but whether it 'comes together' or not is the ultimate indeterminacy. This, the unplannable, the unpredictable in tennis – as in all sport, and life. On the day timing seems to break all the simple, positivist notions of study. Does it fall into so-called post-modernist thought? Nothing guaranteed. To time the two timings to be together is more like an act of luck. Chance. Once you have done all possible to prepare, you may as well pray it comes off at the right time: that the timing of the timing of the timings is timely. After it is all over, you can say well that day wasn't mine – or that day was my lucky day.

A sort of chance. Tennis, as everyone knows is a game of great skill. The play of experts. The timing of the strokes is a result of constant practice and an innate skill which together give the player such control, such mastery that his performance, his display of his power is such that the audience is in awe. We thrill at this spectacle of mastery. Added to this is the timing , strategy, sheer human concentration and mind over matter, this extreme self-control once again is of such dramatic quality that we are moved, we identify with the player, we thrill with him , we ache with him-we witness a profoundly human drama in which one person will end vanquished in every way by an opponent who , on that day at least, possessed the stronger will-power. The game may display such bravery, stoicism, effort, refusal to surrender, than when it ends, as it must in one winner and one loser, we spontaneously applause them both. They are both heroes. Cathectic.

With such language it seems obvious that tennis, as the paradigmatic combative sport must, at some unconscious level, operate as a cultural psychological displacement for mortal battles of yore. Tennis is a sanitised fight to the death. As thrilling, tense, traumatic as any forum combat – but no blood spilt – at least not literally.

But could tennis serve a more profound purpose as well? The game displays such human control, such necessity, such a manifestation of cause-effect, that it may well celebrate the conquest of chance, of fate, of a determining god, and the humanistic triumph of man we have constantly celebrated since the sixteenth century. The modern west culturally denies chance – it does not fit our scientific ethos, based as that is on man's control of nature and himself. Things are determined; and we understand the laws of all such determinations and with many of them we are part of the determining cause. But the more we look at timing the more clearly we see that ultimately the player is not in control; the outcome is beyond him.

So tennis ultimately displays the triumph of the

ineffable; that, even in this man-made, perfectly 'controlled', rule-bound, game of hitting the ball, a simple abstraction from the complexities of life that it's a relief for all to escape into it – especially the viewers. Tennis is a spectacle-sport – see Guy Debord's 1967 book *The Society of the Spectacle* which offers and acute depiction of modern westerners' disposition to look, not to act. Perhaps we could go further and say that the seduction of being sated and satisfied by watching yet another spectacle is the greatest weapon of the modern state. We, not the official players, are the key players. We are indispensible – it would not proceed without us; and it is for us, for our gratification – proud collectively at what we, mankind, can achieve : the protestant ethic – with hard work, constant training and depriving ourselves of a luxurious life, we can control this little ball inside this court – we are master.

But we are not. It deceives us – even our unconscious!

It also shows that the common distinction between a game of chance (cards) and a game of skill is inadequate. Certainly tennis is a game of skill and spectacle – but this does not oppose it to chance. They are not exclusive of each other (were games of chance a non-western creation and preoccupation, and games of skill a western one?). So chance exists in them all; and skill exists in some of them. The Australian coin game of 'Two-up' is the paradigm of the play of pure chance. We do not, culturally, in the west, respect chance games, only skill games – the former are either illegal or low class, or judged as a leisure-activity for women or the elderly. Spectacle sport culturally remains important: players are cultural heroes; full of commitments, loyalties (including nationalisms) – all this not because it is a good thing to look at – but for deep psychological reasons – human mastery, skill and nothing left to chance.

In tennis, that is, in games of skill, chance is considered close to irrelevant, almost not proper. Thus, when you win a point in tennis, by accident, when, for example, the ball hits the net and roles over – it is common for the player to acknowledge this with a brief form of apology. Legitimate chance ends after the initial toss of the coin for choice of serve or end – and a toss of a coin is so symbolic of chance – so much a declaration that with this gesture all chance ends; the umpire then takes up his position and 'play' begins, that is, a competition of talent , skill, masterliness.

But before we become too complacent with any 'conclusion', it would be wise to turn to another wise author; wise beyond reason, Georges Perec. In his remarkable fable of our times, *W, or The memory Childhood* (1975), I am thinking of those terrible three pages of chapter thirty-six:

> A W athlete has scarcely any control over his life. He has nothing to expect from the passing of time. Neither the alternation of days and nights nor the seasons' round will come to his aid ... The life of an

athlete of W is but a single, endless, furious striving, a pointless, debilitating pursuit of that unreal instant when triumph can bring rest ... Run, run on cinders, run through the marshes, run in the mud. Run, jump, put the shot ... Run ! Jump ! Crawl! ... On your knees! Submerged in a world unchecked, with no knowledge of the Laws that crush him ... the W athlete does not know where his real enemies are (Perec 1989).

Can that be us?

Timing and Nietzsche

According to Nietzsche, the philosopher is neither eternal nor historical, but untimely, always untimely. Untimely meaning not belonging to his time; neither a simple reflection of his period, nor responsible to it (in the sense of only to it). He is above, beyond, independent of his time and place in history.

The philosopher has autonomy. Nor eternal – we do not return all the time, or from time to time to the same philosophical points, arguments, conclusions. There is not one simple, eternal philosophic position, which some 'philosophers' assume: any decent real philosopher would reach the same conclusion – because it is nothing other than an application of an eternal logic, true in all times and places. These two positions are the opposite of each other: one reflecting a simple positivist historicism – everyone, philosophers included, are of their times. The other reflects the conventional transcendentalism of western philosophy – that philosophy is entirely divorced from a social, cultural, political setting in reality – from real life, and emanates a universal truth. He represents nothing other than the universal, eternal 'Mind' at work.

Being untimely, as Nietzsche stresses, rejects both positions. Without being a universal man, he is of no time, no particular time or times. Neither the two options offered nor some form of dialectical synthesis belonging to no historical period, is an alternative possibility. A neither-nor, a bothand. He is of many places and times, and of none in particular. He does not fit. He is not easily labeled, slotted into some descriptive pigeon-hole. Nor is he 'a man for all seasons' – fitting in always. No, his non-historicism and his non-universalism leave him craggy.

Thus the second meaning of 'untimely' – he is never expected (he is not clearly one thing or another to enable him to be expected). People are always unprepared for him. He is too early and/or too late. There is no season for the philosopher. And he is unwelcome, always, anywhere. What he has to say is not of the times, nor can it be. His thoughts are always alien, disconcerting, against the times. To be timely would means he is not a philosopher. Does this also suggest that being so untimely he is fated to fail? Can people ever understand him? Do they ever want to understand him? The philosopher is, thus, surely, based on Nietzsche himself. And Zarathustra?

So, ultimately the question of the philosopher is the problem of the relationship between the wise person and the masses, captives of their narrow times. Who wins? No one?

We can relate this meaning of untimeliness and the function of the philosopher to an earlier thought above about the tennis player who is not responsible, whose sense of match-play is such that they are unconcerned with strategic timing, who will play the ball always the same way and that is with flair, with recklessness, with abandon, who plays for the joy of it rather than for a win. Could we say such a player is the philosopher of tennis? Not bound by the rules, roles common of the day – a battle to the end, a means/ends struggle, dedication to the task, rejecting all this is not of the times. Playing for playing sake; the thrill, brilliance of the game is its own end – there is no means/end distinction.

Is this, maybe, the picture of the child? As Gadamer reads Nietzsche. The third transformation is that into the spirit of the child; it is the spirit of innocence, of play, of a complete lack of awareness of time, of a life completely for the moment, of being quickly consoled for all missed opportunities. According to Zarathustra this is the highest form of the spirit (see Gadamer 2003). Yes, it is for the moment (that is the 'Leconte' as model of non-timing); no planning, no regret (is this what is suggested by 'quickly consoled for missed opportunities'?). 'Lack of awareness of time' is an interesting thought. Is one so occupied, and satisfied, with the momentary pleasures that one needs no past or future, one has no consciousness of either? It is not quite that time stands still, or stops; it is that Time itself, as a concept, as a reality, is absent, irrelevant, meaningless. This kind of play creates, demands, Timelessness. So, thoughts like 'who is going to win this match after another one hour or so?' is inconceivable. If one does ask this, one has been distracted – an impure thought! A distracted person is no longer 'in the moment'.

Edith Piaf's famous song, *Non, je ne regrette rien*, 'I regret nothing' resonates here: okay, there was an opportunity – but I missed it perhaps through my own fault – a pity, but that's life, no regrets. So, never get caught in the past, nor concerned for the future; one merely lives for the present (which thereby loses its normal sense as a temporal line has evaporated). Gadamer again, 'Zarathustra's message: to learn acceptance'. Is this the 'the innocence of the child'?

Again this seems related to Gadamer's conclusion:

The free spirits, the higher men, are such searchers and sufferers, who cannot cast off the spirit of gravity. It is the ease of the child, its ease for forgetting, its timelessness, it is arising in the there of the moment, it is playing that surpasses them all. It is like a song. Song is human existence (Dasein) – not something intentional, indeed, beyond all disclosing of intention, beyond all 'un-concealing', something rather lying behind that fulfills itself entirely in itself. What is past, no spirit of revenge, no desire to hold (Gadamer 1988).

Timelessness. The idea has several dimensions. First as here, the notion of innocence, of the child; taken with (obsessed?) with the present moment, it becomes all – no past, no future, no plans, no regrets. The moment is the sole reward, activity. All temporal ideas of time collapse into a oneness, the now. Being timely, or untimely no longer makes sense; the question of timing is irrelevant. Second, timelessness representing the eternal, such as in the dominant western idea of Truth – one truth and it is timeless, absolute. The same here as there, now and then. Transcendental. This is opposed to notions of relative knowledge – differences according to different cultures, epistemes, metaphors: here truth is historical, temporally anchored. Truth will always be timely, of the times. A further opposition, related only partly to the relativism just discussed, is the idea of truth as timed, timed well, made timely because of its untimeliness. This is Vaclav Havel's idea of truth – that which is needed for the occasion. Appropriate, not in the sense of fitting the times, but geared consequentially, in terms of a desired outcome. Politics as the timing of a truth. For this moment or situation, it would be said, this rather than that is called for. Timing as positive intervention. Nothing could seem to be further removed from timelessness than this. And yet! There is some connection between the first sense of timeless – that of the child, and this denial of a timeless knowledge, or morality. They both are concerned with the present: for the one, only the present moment is relevant; for the other, the nature of the present moment is of all importance. One is unconcerned with notions of an absolute, timeless position, with its consistency, or with precedents of yesterday or with a distant future. One wants to know what one should do now, in the precisely given circumstance. Each moment is perhaps unique; one is responsible only to that. One will be judged accordingly. Timing is everything. Or, to the child, timing is nothing. So, concern with the present moment can produce either the extreme the irresponsible, playful child or its opposite, the most 'pragmatic', ruthless, amoral activist. Both, in different ways, turn their backs on history, on any larger view of things, on an other worldliness. They live for the moment.

The third sense of timelessness relates to Freud's idea of the unconscious being timeless. This is meant specifically as a contrast to the conventional western notion of time as linear, of the uniform, neutral clock/historical linear time. If it is not that, it is assumed by Freud and others, it is not time, it is timeless. Being timeless, the unconscious has an eternal quality about it; it is always present, at least potentially there; it cannot be erased; the past is there, now and in the future – in this sense, the notion of tense is cancelled. We live in the ever-present past; the future will repeat the past. This form of timelessness, therefore, highlights the past; the eternal past – quite different from the other two forms of timelessness. Living in the past involves the unconscious being ever-ready to be triggered by an event in the present to catalyst a trace from the past. The timeless, unconscious means we live neither in a pure now nor in a pure then – but in a fusion of the two: beyond simple notions of exclusive historical units. Because the unconscious operating as it does, our lives are mixed. You could say that its timelessness does not remove it from historical time; rather it over-ties it to history – twice. The past and the present, and the past and the future are inextricably and messily conjoined. Or, one could say, which Freud may or may not have said explicitly, that this feature and function of the unconscious forces us to revise our over simple notions of linear time. He laid the path for us.

But this language perhaps remains unnecessarily close to our tradition of linearity – in one special way – the implicit and necessary assumption that something (it may be the unconscious) is always there, uniform in its readiness, availability. Something akin to the contemporary penchant to refer to 'the level playing field, economic rationalists and free-trading politicians', or to 'common-sense'?

Let's change the language: instead of referring to the timelessness of the unconscious, we could refer to its Timing. Timing emphasises its periodic, even haphazard, occasional, uneven appearance. It comes – then goes. It does not hang about. The unconscious in this light, is Timing, is the unexpected, sudden bringing together (or brought-together) of two events. It therefore has all the qualities of Timing as previously elaborated. What is specific to it, however, is the meeting, quite unplanned and unplannable, between an actuality and a memory (a psychic wound), the good or bad consequence of this shaping other actualities. One could call this timing the punctuation of the unconscious, its emphasis, its toning, colouring – provided we do not think of the unconscious as continuous with occasional spurts. There is no Unconscious – except when it is Timed into existence by some particular event stimulating some particular memory and producing some particular affect. This is the Unconscious – Timing and nothing else. We could imagine the unconscious over a period of time, collectively, as composed like a mosaic or collage of these affects – ready to be timed or already timed. Primed. So the Unconscious is not like a level playing field, a continuity. It is unevenness – composed of differences which make a difference. When and why all this appears, erupts, is beyond human control. It is a matter of chance – even though there may be some pattern hypothetically discoverable (because of repetition compulsion) in the responses.

Business and timing

Without forcing the language we could compare the businessman to the tennis player in a variety of ways. As we do this, distinctions emerge.

Strategic – a key word. We will begin with excellence again. The businessman needs a vision – a long term sense of goal involving a postponement of rewards and a willingness to take large risks. This needs guts and confidence in himself, in his own judgment. He could lose all because he is risking a lot. In this sense, it is a gamble. Few are able to do this. Business is structurally geared to short-term results, short –term rewards – caution – for example, banks lending money, accountants annual balance. Is balance more important here than elsewhere – in sport or politics for example? But it cannot survive for a long term if sacrificing short term. The two need to go together. Again the coordination of the two is another aspect of Timing and strategy. To know when to be cautious, retreat, do nothing. To know when to risk something, when and where a new opportunity exists or may exist. To be bold, take others by surprise, to think big; or to withdraw, cut losses, reduce outlay. Strategy ultimately involves coordinating short- and long-term goals and activities – and can fail if either is faulty or if the two are not closely reinforcing. They need to fit each other.

'Appropriate' again becomes a key word. It cannot be measured, calculated, only sensed, intuited. Although a reasoning process can be used in reaching what is to be considered appropriate – in the circumstances. But what does it entail? Is there something we can describe called appropriateness? Of course it can be wrong, or become inappropriate if times change. Things no longer fit as they did before. So, appropriate is not restricted to things done, to actions – no, appropriateness implies timed fit. One fits the time. But that expression could be misleading. It is better to say 'fit the circumstances' where that word clearly implies spatial, temporal and contentfull. That is, the circumstance refers short-hand to a particular event as it emerges historically; for example the recession in Australia in the early 1990s – not any or an essential recession, even though similarities will of course be there. Some associative words: in context, apposite, pertinent, applicable, to the point, well directed, proper (sic), suitable, fitting, apt; in accordance with, in keeping with, commensurate, congruent, conforming, in step, in phase, in tune, synchronised, matching, natural, in place, felicitous.

Notice how easily being appropriate can slide into notions of 'proper' or 'natural'. Whilst being either of these surely entails being also appropriate the reverse certainly does not necessarily hold. By this I mean that natural/proper must involve, infer, assume a timeless quality, that something is the right and 'proper' thing to do or to accompany something else Something absolute. A law: one must, one must not. Always – in all circumstances. If one does not comply with such a stricture then one will pay the consequence: one will fail, err, sin – be unnatural or improper.

So, appropriate must be, ought to be preferably restricted to things less than absolute. The expression 'fit and proper' seems to have both qualities about it, and so can be ambiguous: on the one hand it suggests an automatic application of a rule or law, an 'of course', there can be no other; on the other hand it can suggest a judgment made after some deliberation – 'yes, this seems right for the particular occasion'. It may even suggest that an alternative judgment is feasible and not inappropriate(!). To fit the occasion has a casualness about it; there is no interdiction involved. Something horizontal not vertical about it. So, how does one reach a decision whether something is or is not appropriate for the occasion: that it fits well, or is right?

It is not necessarily a retrospective pragmatic judgment – that something actually 'worked'; one can and often does, prematurely, commit oneself: yes, this seems right, let's give it a go. One may know from experience, of course, that certain things are more or less relevant. But there is a suggestion that one is flexible in approach; that one knows things, circumstances vary and that one has to act accordingly. Appropriate as 'apt' captures this aspect: from Middle French *apter* to adapt and now: to make fit, adapt to, to suit. This is fitting in two ways: a) it emphasises variability of task and result and b) it highlights the human component – something is initiated, created, made to work. Everything removed from some theological or juridical model. Nothing is dictated. There is no necessity at least in terms of content, a particular solution, fit; a felt necessity only to discover, create an appropriate response, or, if you wish, a need to achieve the goal you set or the one imposed. More a chance, a punt, a gamble.

To John Sambell, the already mentioned banker, appropriate means a combination of two things: (1) looking to the past experience – and knowing that certain things tend to happen, or always happen, and identifying what was successful last time; that is, to identify repetitions; be aware of the past but then; (2) appreciating what is different this time. People who make mistakes tend to assume that repetitions do not occur; that things will be different this time; especially that we have better tools of analysis now and that we will not make the same mistakes again. But tools of analysis are only inventions of economists and they each have their own. What is more common is a simple projection of the present onto the future; tomorrow will be 'more of today'.

To see an opportunity, you need the talent for reading the signs – for analysing the figures, for projecting. Is that the difference between the businessman and the tennis player? The good businessman is constantly reading the future, the poorer only reading the present. The need to translate current 'facts' into future probabilities. The naive or foolishly optimistic crudely projects an ideal present into the future – as if nothing were to be changed. Thus the mistakes and failures of the late '80s. What works today does not necessarily work the same tomorrow. Is there a time gap between the rewards/returns of a business move which is not there in tennis?

Murdoch, for example, has invested highly in Sky Television, losing money for the last five years. Yet provided he can survive this period of losses, his profits will likely be huge. Now, you cannot lose points and games in tennis as a means of a greater win down the line. What superficially seems similar is the differential value of points or games. One point won can give you the game or the set, even match. Or lose it. One needs to know the overall situation, schema of things to appreciate the high or low value of moves. Nothing is uniform or fixed in tennis. Similar in business, depending on the circumstances, the same action may be great or disastrous. In each 'game' a move is more than a move, it is a 'timed move', a 'located move'. It is loaded, variably.

Is a deferment a central part of business which has no parallel in tennis? And, as with any deferment, no outcome is guaranteed. Things can change along the way. There is deferment in tennis in the sense that the reward comes say after a three-hour match or at the end of a two week tournament. This is merely shorter but still isomorphic with a two or five year delay before profits flow in a business enterprise. A different time span . But the difference is still there. Strategically you do not decide to lose a set along the way – as a necessary part of a plan, as a timely defeat to ensure eventual victory. But you may do this in business; calculating inevitable losses as fitting. But should they be seen as solely and purely 'losses'? Should we redefine them as only apparent defeats –

like the military decision to lose small battles in order to win the war. They are carefully timed 'expenses' – not just any loss, or any amount planned and seen as successful expenditures. Like a rite de passage. A trial; a test; an ordeal – one has to fight and conquer the fierce dragon in order to reach the treasure.

So, tennis and business may be comparable after all – but the match is the wrong unit of comparison. This needs to be seen merely as the last battle after months of training and sweat. They both postpone their gratifications, planning necessarily to suffer along the way – one by an expenditure of money without immediate returns, the other by an expenditure of physical effort without immediate return.

Opportunity is not only something that exists out there because of some conjunction of forces. It can also be fabricated inside and made to be felt outside – irrespective of other circumstances. This is the regularly repeated sales pitch: announcing a SALE – a reduction in prices (usually minimal) and note, one that 'can never be repeated'. So, not only is the time right, and is the opportunity everyone allegedly has been waiting for – it is more – it is announced as the only opportunity – thus one that cannot be missed because if you miss this you miss them all. So added to the expedience of the timing – one would be a fool to miss the occasion – it is now or never.

Timing plays a double role here. a) it is now and for a short period of time only, that one has an opportunity to buy cheaply. That is the conventional

Sale. It's now! It wasn't on last month; it won't be next month – but for the time being – now – it is it. The opportunity is not to be missed. And this is perfectly honest and truthful. b) this present timing is a unique timing. The moment is sui generis. Once for ever. Now or never.

Timing as an Economy is not an economy of time – like saving time. It is the coordination of time, place and action (an investment) in the way best suited, geared to produce a desired result – here maximum profit, or often minimum loss The economy is the tidiness, neatness, efficiency of fit, the smoothness, the ease, the 'naturalness' of the union. As with perfect timing of strokes in sport, the economy of business timing (or in life!) is its apparent effortlessness. Picking the right time seems doing the 'proper' thing, the appropriate thing. It is smooth, flowing. One pulls with the punch, or flows with the tide. You do not fight against impossible odds – it is not a battle in that sense – though a lot of military-style strategy in thought and preparation will have gone into it. All the bits seem to fit, go together. As the Oxford dictionary defines 'coordination' (in one sense) – a harmonious combination of agents or functions towards the promotion of a result. Timing is a mental activity above everything else – it is also psychological.

To defer and timing.

In certain activities, to defer is the totality of timing.

Think of humour, oral humour. To tell a joke, or even to narrate a tall story, the essence of the skill, the perfect execution of it, is a deliberate holding back. It may be nothing more than a momentary pause for a few seconds – and then the punch line or even single word. Without the pause the joke would fail or at least fall flat. What does this silence, this absence, this nothing, this interregnum do? It is certainly not an additional thing like an unnecessary mannerism, a style, an additional flourish; it is central, inherent, part of the last line itself.

The audience is complicit with its function. It works because the audience knows what it means. It make them expectant of an end. The momentary silent pause is not unlike foreplay, to excite the 'other' to get their humour-juices working, to tell them they are now on the cusp of a funny climax.

Is it readiness, the creating or a readiness that is involved with this delay, this deferral?

Timing as coordination.

Cooking a meal is a perfect example of this aspect of timing. The task essentially being to complete the preparation of all the cooking with everything ready as the same time. One has to plan to do certain steps of a dish or begin another dish before or after others on the knowledge that different times are needed to cook different things. To make mistakes in timing entails over-cooking some things, over-cooling of others, a waste of time waiting with nothing to do. This is related to but different from the timing involved say in building a house. There it is known that certain things are prerequisites for others: you cannot have Z before you have completed Y. No-one but an idiot could err. Though if not enough time has been allocated to do/ complete Z, then a waste of time can occur.

Restaurant cooking constitutes a paradigm of complex coordination of timing. A leading Australian chef/restaurateur, Stephanie Alexander, describes it in a long discussion with me in 1992:

> Timing is critical, absolutely essential ... The skill of the kitchen is to make sure that all those various components are properly timed and come together at the right time which has to be a suitable interval from the time the person ordered. The whole evening runs on time .... As soon as the order hits the kitchen we read it out and we say it's one souffle, one that and one something or other followed by one duck, one barramundi and one chicken ... The cook knows that the chicken will take 45 minutes, the duck ten minutes to cook ... The first thing we do is to estimate when the meal is going to be served; we like to feel that anyone ordering by say, 8 o'clock, will have their main course by 9 o'clock ... By that time they will have had a little appetiser, an entree, and they will have had that cleared away, and by then their main course arrives at their table ... Obviously there are various things that can go wrong with this. We may have customers who want to eat particularly slowly, and as long as they com-

municate that, that's fine; you may have a particularly dreadful night which happens often on a Saturday night when up to eighty-five percent of the customers arrive within ten minutes of each other, and there's no way in the world that even a genius could cook say eighty main courses within ten minutes of each other ... Some people take longer to order so they don't hurry those – they let them sit there having pre-dinner drinks.---Some customers, when they come in and sit down, say, 'We want a long, leisurely evening; we don't want to be fed too fast' ... We try to encourage that sort of communication. Some people suddenly decide to go for a walk between courses, or they may want to have a cigarette ... If the customer communicates a timing wish, it will be respected. Others obviously want to snap into getting their evening started; we are inclined to let the two's go first because they often don't have that much to say to each other ... There are some preparations in the kitchen for which precise timing is absolutely critical. For some, a minute is critically important, for example a souffle: there's a minute before it's ready, a minute when it's ready and a minute when it's too far gone ... It's very much split-second timing.

The minute we start putting food on plates ('platting') we know we can't do it again for ten minutes. It takes that length of time to dress twelve plates, which is what we send out at a time, say a table of five ... As the customer has each course, his docket will drop to the wire immediately below. It's all very simple and visual; you don't need to know a code to read it. Waiters ... may say 'no, they are going very slowly'. So we will leave them and take up another table. We link them all together at one time and write 05 and then automatically write 15 on the next batch of dockets ... You can't afford too many mistakes. It's not just an awareness of timing that counts; we've got equipment that can do things in three minutes, because of the heat it generates, which you can't do at home ... We cook our ducks for seven minutes then we rest them in a hot dish and for the next five minutes is part of our calculation, and that extra five makes all the difference ... So timing is just absolutely the name of the game.

Of course, the preparation, the mise-en-place, takes place all day long. Every piece of food that is going on a plate that night has been handled ... You just can't start preparing when they order the food or the customer would have to wait an hour and a quarter to be fed.

Mistiming can sometimes come about through our mistake or through the behaviour of the customer ... Sometimes it's more serious than other times ... If it is that someone has got a souffle ready too soon there's nothing I can do. It has to be thrown in the bin; they'll have to start again and that means that the sardines have to be thrown out also but it doesn't mean that the salmon has to be thrown out because it's cold. On the other hand, if a customer suddenly goes for a walk or goes to the toilet and doesn't return for five minutes that can be a drama. But mistiming is usually because someone has mucked up the cooking process ... It's a fine balance between making sure you're operating and allowing a reasonable margin of error ...

You have to be able to thrive on the pressure. I've had wonderful cooks, sensitive with lovely ideas, but who fall apart in the service. They just cannot operate with so many instructions coming at them at once. Those people are not with us any more. It's a sad thing.

Timing and psychoanalysis.

Essential and central is the unanimous opinion of the value of timing in the psychoanalytical session. We can immediately see references and similarities from elsewhere, but there seems something unique to the therapeutic session. It is a discourse sui generis. Timing is initially described as the particular moment chosen by the analyst to articulate an interpretation. It is understandable for beginners, and still a constant temptation for the experienced, to want to announce an insight, an association, an interpretation as soon as it is conceived.

But premature revelation, no matter how accurate, can be counter-productive: it will automatically give offence, and more significantly produce a flush of defenses which may then take years to undo. So, timing in this centrally, strategic way is essentially a deferment, a delay, a postponement of information until the moment it is considered right to tell it. The appropriate moment – that word resonates yet again.

So what is the appropriate moment that constitutes good timing in this situation? That which it is considered by the analyst to be the time when the patient will be most receptive of the news. Again the same key word, readiness. Being receptive or being ready implies not simply a conscious or intellectual preparedness (a too-willing verbal agreement with an observation is without value) but something vague like 'the unconscious being ready' – which means that the interpretation will be absorbed, accepted and used. A 'move' will be made by the patient – that's proof that the timing was right.

The problem then is to tell the time, know the signs, that the occasion is ripe. Sheer intuition based on experience. It may be impossible to be more precise than that. It is not easy; senior analysts admit. It is described as reading the signs within the self; the reciprocity, and nonreciprocity, of analysis is constantly highlighted. If you listen to the patient carefully you will hear him/her coming to the same conclusion as you. He slowly gets around to it. Ideal timing of an interpretation is getting as close as possible to the same time that the patient is arriving at the same conclusion. The analyst merely helps her over the last small step. Like letting go of the twowheel bike – just when the child has the confidence and ability to finally ride by himself. You cannot rush this moment. Patience. One has to wait.

One knows you are right at times immediately; such as when the patient virtually interprets it along with the analyst, like saying 'yes that's what I've been thinking, but I hadn't quite put it into words'. The two are one. Initial judgments may be wrong – or premature. The strength of a response may initially suggest timing was wrong; but subsequently the analyst may decide that in fact the timing was after all good. Judgments are never final.

Timing, of course, is not something that happens or becomes relevant just now and then. It is pertinent all the time. One could say timing is the constant punctuation of the session and of the entire life of an analysis. Timing like music. It constitutes the beat, the rhythm, the tempo, even the very lyrics of analysis. It records and tests when to listen, when to ask questions, when to comment, when, and for how long, to allow a silence to endure (silence may be an impotent moment, or a creative one). Timing, both good and bad, operates all the time. Analysis is timing. Analysis and music: a fugue, a theme and variations. Elaborations of an initial theme. Reworking of a theme that takes the theme further; otherwise nothing other than repetition, but not just the same old stuff. It may need many repetitions before seeing, and confirming that it is a pattern. A certain simple rhythm is appropriate at the beginning; it builds trust for one thing. Repetition is needed to discover a pattern. After that the tempo varies and becomes complex. If the rhythm remains too steady for too long, however – a lullaby – you need to change; no work, no analysis is being done. One should never jump in too quickly; you may make an inappropriate interpretation. You need to curb your own desire to reveal, to show-off, to relieve self and patient. The analyst must be patient – with both self and other.

If timing is the beat, the very orchestration of

analysis, one needs to know what was the unconscious orchestration of that orchestration. What timed the timing! This question highlights the notion that timing in analysis should not be seen simply as the clever, neutral manipulation of the discourse. The analyst is being analysed, indirectly at least, and preferably with constant awareness by the analyst. With transference and counter-transference both operating, the unconscious construction of the timing , whilst there, is likely to be always quite beyond human ability to delineate or understand. Just as it is understandable, and necessary, for the question 'why did you say that?' to represent the analytic quest, the desire to expose the repressed, the hidden motivations of an individual – thus showing the correct dissatisfaction with surface phenomena, with the apparent, the manifest content – so an awareness of a timing of the timing, an analysis of the analysis, reminds us again of our inevitable, hidden determinants. And a nice reminder that the analyst is not omnipotent. She is not in control of the session. Who/what controls it is ultimately ineffable.

Timing is an art – a skill that can be bettered with training and experience – but it still remains an art not a science. It is not generalisable. It is particular to each patient – even that has layers: the macro – representing the entire period, maybe years, of a person's analysis and then the micro, each and every session comprises a mini-whole in itself. Thus the stress on ignoring memory (such as what happened last session) or general desires (to announce an insight, to help the patient). One must attend to the now, the present.

There is chance in analysis. On first consideration we would not imagine that, unlike in say politics or business or life generally, chance would play little role, we would think. There is no chance in the unconscious, Freud constantly reminds us; everything has a meaning, an explanation – unlike, he adds, the chanciness of external reality.

Although, as Derrida argues, the distinction between chance and determinism may not be as obvious as we would assume. In the analytic situation there is also no chanciness in the sense that an analyst should not take a punt. He does not play by chance. And yet!

It can be said that chance is central here as well, though from a different perspective. The analyst is on the lookout for the chance remark, the unexpected. He needs that, it is desired, because it may provide the opportunity to understand something. A slip of the tongue, the parapraxis, is the epitome of the chance event. Chance allows a move in interpretation to be made, and perhaps a move by the patient. Quite a casual chance comment lightly tossed out by the analyst may create dramatic responses from the patient. It may be possible, sometimes, to explain why this was so; that, at the unconscious level, a knowing collusion between the two people was in operation. There is more than merely the conventional form to communication. Again, it may be that it remains not only unexpected but inexplicable. Chance, even here, can never be totally denied. The analyst in turn may appear surprised. A patient, repeating an over-familiar story may, suddenly, tell it differently, with a new nuance. Something has been added, unawares to his understanding. It emerges, unannounced, frequently to the surprise of both parties. A movement has been made from an intellectual to an experiential understanding.

Chance in politics or business, more often than not, is not desired. One tries to plan ahead, to forecast the future, to expect, or hope, that things will continue on the present path (if things are going well) or a hoped-for projection of the future. That is, one attempts to forecast future changes thus avoiding being taken by surprise by a chance change, that is one prefers not to experience unexpected eruptions. One cannot plan for chance; and, when/or if it comes, one copes with it as best one can; it may present an obstacle to overcome, or a sudden opportunity which you seize as best you can.

In analysis, however, a future forecast is inconceivable; one can and must operate only in the present. One patiently waits for a chance remark; one cannot time that. Analysis is nothing other than the search and wait for the emergence of the repressed – and this is a chance affair, and as elsewhere, a chance for the analyst to profit, to be rewarded. Hypothetically at least, whatever the chance turns out to be, it is to the analyst always timely. Nothing can be unfavourable. Everything constitutes an opportunity to gain an insight. It is up to the talent of the analyst whether good is made of it or not.

So, analysis is a game of chance. Tokens of little value are the mundane, rational, conscious contributions in the discourse. One cannot move far, or at all, with that currency. Tokens of high value, however, are the occasional chance remarks. They are remarkable. Big moves can be made with their use. The game ends with their successful deployment whereby nothing is left to chance; all is satisfactorily understand. It is clear that a game of chance need not be a gamble. Work and play conjoin in analysis: 'hard play' is a useful thought there is nothing easy, casual about it. It is imaginative, operating with elasticity – using room (time) to manoeuvre (based on an interview with a Melbourne psychoanalyst).

Timing and interpretation.

A review in the *London Review of Books*, 7 February 2019, concerns a study of institutional racism in the British police force. One policeman, who, having complained to senior officers about transparent racism in one particular case, was soon after overlooked for promotion. He resigned from the force. Two years later, he was suddenly accused of indecent assault of a minor thirty years previously. His solicitor (the writer of the review) quickly called into question the truth of the allegation because 'the timing of the decision to investigate him was suspicious: the man was at this point seeking election as a local councilor for the Labour Party'. In court the accusation was proven to be a total fabrication.

It would be an interesting experiment for readers of this book to look at their own behaviour over the years, and see how, perfectly innocently, they automatically time when, and when not, they tell their partner or their work boss certain matters. We all behave with that form of basic sense, responsibility, caution, respect. That is an essential part of being part of human society. Timing is one inherent component of civilisation. Imagine its hypothetical absence.

As any social trait or value can be abused, so can timing, as has been illustrated through this chapter. So, another interesting Sherlock Holmes experiment would be to wonder why a public person does something at some particular time, and not at another. Timing can readily reveal the motivation behind a need.

Timing and art.

The paradox of the avant-garde is that you have to be different to be considered successful; but to be different means you are not understood often and so you cannot be successful. Ideally, if you strongly wish for recognition, you need to make your work only marginally different – it needs to be recognizable. A little space but not too much. But a 'real' artist should never be manipulative or opportunist. It is a consequence not a goal.

A second paradox. To be different means, in fact, that you are the first, you need to be first in time to do X otherwise you will not appear to be different. To recover, restore, resurrect something old, past, not in time or timely – and by adding something to that particular past, by 'framing' it differently, you are seen as new. Newness is constituted by a particular oldness. A new is always a re-new of something always already there, as Derrida would say. You return to the past, restate what is there which can never be a simple repetition, you return to the now with a new old. Timing is essential – you have to have done that something first to be successful.

In 1982 Geoff Lowe had a great success with an exhibition. He saw it coming; he was confident that he had tapped something in the air. He was expressing something new, of the time. He was clearly timely. So, critical and commercial success. Two years later, much to his surprise, his next show was a flop – in all ways. He was considered saying nothing new – though he still believed he was. This may happen; but it does not happen always; something else may well be the critical matter. Think of Picasso, Kandinsky, Pollack, just to begin.

Not that art has to be timely all the time; often it needs to be untimely (see Nietzsche: an artist against his times). You could say that for his first show his timing was perfect: it matched what a public felt –

even though this perhaps had never been articulated: he expressed what people were ready and keen to say. Thus, they immediately recognised what he was saying. This is similar to the analytic situation in which the analyst tries to offer an interpretation at the very moment that the patient is ready to say the same thing. Both gel: synchronicity: the two come together.

So, we have three areas of activity with a similar theme. Timing is the temporal matching of two parties. They are on the same wavelength in a manner which allows, or insists, that a mutual appreciation of something is reached, (is climaxed) together. The ideal of timing – in three modes: the analyst reaches a useful interpretation of the patient's condition: this is held back until the patient is ready to see this, experientially not merely intellectually. This is a process of repetition, of theme and variations – but with one party in a more knowledgeable position than the other and hence operating, to some degree or other, as both a catalyst of the other whilst resisting 'exposing' or 'revealing' itself – until the other can appreciate the revelation. They reach the conclusion together.

A paradigm of perfect timing. Lovers begin more as equals – though this may vary through the process of making love – meaning the mutual stimulation and increased excitement until both parties come together.

As with the analytic situation there is some varying degree of consciousness and unconsciousness in the process of getting two parties to reach a match.

For some perfect fit to be created. This does not come automatically – it has to be worked at – some are more naturally skilled than others; it also takes experience. There can be no rules for a good operation.

A routinised procedure is doomed to fail. This inevitable failure is perhaps because of the nature of the revelation or climax (and of the process reaching that) – and by this is meant that it is neither simply a physical or an intellectual, or an emotional process. It is one in which everything is involved necessarily. All is enmeshed. And partly because of this we feel obliged to reach for words like 'intuition' in describing the talents and attributes and mental/physical processes which are engaged. It is clearly 'beyond reason' in the analytic setting as it is 'beyond simple physicality in the erotic setting. Within the person as between the partners a unit, a oneness is involved. Timing, in its perfection, is the removal of space, of boundaries (psychic or physical) and the emergence, generation of a oneness.

In art, work is created which somehow accords with the as yet unexpressed sentiments – no simple word is available – but again it is a meshing of intellect, emotion, physicality of a public. Here the operation has a separateness about it – the artist appears to operate in isolation – but we could be misled by its physical isolation , ignoring that the artist is not separate from the public and if something vague yet real is 'in the air', the artist is in some communion with the public throughout the operation of the art creation. Communion seems a good word for capturing what happens with ideal timing. Nevertheless, a difference exists. In love and analysis a constant dialogue is in operation throughout a period of concern (in months and years in one, in minutes for the other) – and this is based on physical contact and awareness of each other. Not so with the artist. He is in no position to 'know' who his public will be. In a way, the two parties exist independently of each other. There can be therefore no comparable deferring, stimulating, encouraging – indeed no concrete process going on and aiming at some climax. When the art is displayed there is some degree of innocence on each side (though Lowe insists he knew it was going to be a success – emphatically). There is a sudden revelation, an unveiling, an instant exposure. There normally therefore must be some degree of mutual surprise preceded by a moment of expectation, wonderment, hunch – all in ignorance of the other – what is it going to be? who are they? what will they think?

So, whether there is indeed ideal timing, a perfect fit between the expression of the art and what the public are inchoately feeling, it is one achieved without preparatory work as it were. That is, other than the presence of a cultural climate felt or not to varying degrees by the individuals concerned. No intentionality exists here as to a degree it exists in the two other examples. Even with an opportunist artist all he can do is to attempt to give the public what he thinks they want; he can't go beyond this (like the lover or the analyst) and patiently, expertly prepare them for it, lead them to it, stimulate their desires and interest in a way that they peak at the appropriate moment In the other two situations we could say that the timing was (in part) timed by a human agent; with the artist we can't say anything like this.

The contrast can be expressed in another way as well: with two of them but not with the third, we can say that timing is part and parcel of the entire operation. Timing must not be seen merely in the successful climax, the coming-together on time. It is there all the time in the very 'pacing' of the two main actor's each move, each deferred move is part of the timed preparation for the well-timed end and, in fact, is part of that end – the distinction between means and ends here seems misleading – as elsewhere. If the timing is wrong throughout the process one cannot achieve successful timing at the end – in fact the termination of analysis is deferred as long as timing is wrong; and in love making there is an end for one partner only with inadequate timing. Thus, the expression 'to come prematurely' – untimely. However, with the artist and his public we have no comparable timing during the process. He is not pacing himself – because this aspect of Timing requires more than one party – it is a relationship. The artist is surely engaged with himself (not with anyone outside?) in the process of creation, so, if anything, the artist is timing himself with sketches, in preparation for himself to peak – and then the work of art can be created – not just anytime; the artist has to make himself 'ready'. So readiness acquires a new sense here: it is a private, isolated one irrespective of comparisons with others, it is obvious that the artist has to time himself, prepare himself to – some time or other, (that is, not depending on others) produce the work of art. This may not necessarily follow the more graduated curve of preparedness which the analyst and lover need follow. It may be more erratic. But something has to be done and achieved; no artist can produce a work of art at any time. The idea of timing reminds us that expressions like 'always' and its opposite 'at any time' (ignoring its other opposite 'never') are not equally applicable in all activities (if any!!) – timing precludes both as beyond conception – certain things can occur only at certain times.

Another Melbourne artist, P.M., when asked whether there was a right time or manner to start a new painting, replied, that you can start at any time – but, he emphatically continued, there is a right time to end a painting – otherwise the work gets destroyed, as if you are in a boxing ring, and a heavy-weight boxer is smashing your face to pieces.

C.M., another artist, said this about his work: 'There was a long period in the '70s when I was wandering around in the wilderness. Then in the '80s things started to happen, my work was set on the right track. It is a pretty slow process being a painter, it takes a long time; it's a matter of mastering the medium, getting a handle on the materials and finding out what you want to say. You can't force it, it has to just happen' (*The Age*, May 5, 1992). It happens, as it were, in its own time, not just any time when, for example, the artist wants it to happen. But, of course, as Amor says, the artist has to work towards this readiness. Nothing happens autonomously.

Marcel Duchamp, wit, ironist, and in many ways one of the most radical experimenters in art, contemplated challenging this apparent necessity for correct timing. At least he wrote about it in his diary indicating the radicalness of the very idea – even for him. Whether it was written tongue in cheek we cannot say today – although in a sense everything he attempted was in that mode. However, he wrote about challenging appropriate timing by flaunting it, by insisting that his 'readymades' could be made without readiness, that is, could be created at whim, by chance, indeed, by planning for chance! (for the moment ignoring the paradoxical nature of that expression), it ought to be here. The first and main entry follows:

Specifications for 'Readymades'

By planning for a moment to come (on such a day, such a date such a minute), 'to inscribe a readymade' – the readymade can later be looked for (with all kinds of delays). With this matter of timing, this snapshot effect, like a speech delivered on no matter what occasion but at such and such an hour. It is a kind of 'rendezvous'.

Subsequently Duchamp records that he never quite implemented this.

Everything is located 'in' time – that's clear (or is it?). But everything is in some way 'of' its time. Things came into existence because of its historical time and place. It is, as it were, because it is then and there; otherwise it would be otherwise. Everything is timed in this sense. Not, however, in a totalistic sense, nor in an over-deterministic sense. This is not a causal statement; an earlier reality does not cause a later one; something is not wholly produced by its context (whatever that means – though in the context's broadest possible meaning – it is tautologically true). Nor is anything wholly explicable in terms of something else at the time.

But, that something occurred, that something was produced, is always, in part, because of its timing. A thought, a policy, a work of art, is what it is because it/we/they /the producers could 'take for granted' certain things that had already occurred. Antonio Vivaldi, for example, could compose as he did because of what his earlier fellow Venetians like Gabrielli had already composed. He had no need to risk certain things, to gamble, to experiment, to shock, because those battles, those steps had already been accepted.

Pleasure and its timing.

Pleasure, whatever that means, is something we all strive for – to some degree or other – whether out of human necessity (a drive, à la Freud and Nietzsche) or through some conscious volition. We do not normally try to avoid it – unless we are acting under certain hygienic, moral, religious strictures which say that X, though pleasurable, ought to be avoided – say cream cakes or casual sex.

But it is something we do not (normally) expect all the time: 'life wasn't meant to be just pleasure'. That can be acceptable because, apart from practical problems of obtaining it constantly, there is surely a recognition, somewhere deep in us, that pleasure needs to be 'taken' in relatively small doses, otherwise it would lose its flavour. Pleasure, in other words, is commonly believed to coarsen with excessive use.

Michel Foucault in *The Use of Pleasure*, discusses this issue in classical Greek culture. 'The Strategy of Timeliness' he calls the section, under the broader heading 'the moral probemization of pleasures'. Kairos, the 'opportune' time, was stressed by many including Plato in Laws. The ideal being to know what is needed to be done 'at the right time and in the right amount' (Foucault 1984). The right time, most important to the Greeks, being not only a moral problem but a question of science and technique. The exercise of practical skills, as in medicine, government and navigation, meant not only one must know general principles but also one needs to know the moment when it was necessary to act and exactly how in the particular circumstances. A key element in the virtue of prudence was being able to practice the politics of timeliness in any domain. Morality is also an art of the right time.

There are several scales to that time for pleasure, Greek thought continued: the person's entire life, neither too young nor too old. Pleasure had its season in life; the scale of the year and its season – sex and climate – a complex 'diet' of pleasure ('Diet' in the Oxford Dictionary is 'way of living or thinking; to feed, to regulate the food of a person, in nature or quantity; to regulate oneself'); the right time of day for many reasons 'the evening", for example, because it was the most favourable time for the body, the darkness blotting out unseemly images; and a respectable space of the night intervening before morning's prayers.

The right moment exists for other reasons as well – to distribute pleasures so as not to interfere with other duties, and as requisite recreation after work. Incest is condemned in part because it was not the 'right time' – parents mixing their seeds with children unseasonably.

So, to the Greeks, timing was both a technique (skill and knowledge) and a morality (a self-regulation, a diet, a spacing, distributing, timing, allotting of oneself.) A time and a place for pleasure, as for anything. This assumes that pleasure is an essential part of a good life, but only one part among other essentials. Pleasure, as anything else, needs to be handled as well as possible. To mishandle pleasure means poor pleasure. Pleasure has a quality and a quantity. It interacts with us, and as with any interaction, we can treat ourselves well or badly. If we mistime pleasure it is no longer pleasure. So there is no essential quality, no universal property to unqualified pleasure; something becomes pleasure only when executed well and timely. The skill and occasion are its components, are part of its manufacture. We make pleasure, not take it. Yet pleasure still has some inherent component otherwise we would not know whether it was pleasure or (say) government that we had executed well and timely. Can we go beyond a mere tautology and define it as that which gives us pleasure (or joy)? Yet even that has difficulties because we could say that pleasure can also give us pain – note the constant, universal evocation of pain/pleasure about sex and love.

Too much pleasure in this Grecian perspective, is therefore oddly an oxymoron. Self-contradictory. A paradox. The irony of our modern desires is to believe (and seek) that 'more' of something good is also good, even better; whereas to the Greeks all this suggests the opposite: small is beautiful; a lot is not. Of course, pleasure can suffer from under-use as well. We can be starved of pleasure. Abstinence has no virtue in itself.

The property of pleasure is still left undefined, even under-scribed. We can imagine, however, that certain things may be appropriate to some category of person but not to others. There could be a masculine pleasure which is not appropriate as a feminine pleasure, for example.

It is not simply 'things' like sex or food or wine

which constitute pleasure. Each of these activities/ consumptions are liable to be without pleasure: it is not a matter of, say, any sex or any food. It is a particular quality attainable sometimes in such activities which produce pleasure. Some high quality. Like an excellent execution of an activity. Is perfect timing the essence of a perfect performance? Think first of the making of a fine wine or a fine meal. In the kitchen as in the vineyard and winery we have formula, rather formulae, as new wines and dishes are regularly created. These tell us two things: the appropriate ingredients to be used, and the appropriate time to be taken, or needed, at each stage of the handling and treatment of these ingredients, as they change their form from, say, raw grapes to wine. The particular ingredients with a precise final form of dish decided then, determine (as originally discovered by experience) the time to be taken: two minutes in a wok; one hour in the oven; two years in French oak. The formula, the recipe, the almanac – all for beginners, for the over cautious, for the first time; for the lesson. But no experienced cook/winemaker would think of merely checking the clock. Mechanistic – certainly not. Each would know the necessity for exact timing not uniformly, but each time, for these particular ingredients today or for this harvest. One knows this is a matter of touch, taste, feel, sense, intuition: a judgment quite impossible to ultimately quantify, let alone record, order and dictate to others. It is the quality of such judgments which makes all the difference: be-

tween a poor, reasonable or outstanding product; between a merely competent or a very talented cook or
winemaker; between a task being experienced as little
more than a necessary chore to be done or something
which provides some satisfaction, one which quietly
thrills with pleasure each time at the sheer mastery of
it all. In all these ways, timing is the essence.

So, in considering exactly what gives pleasure have
we unearthed a circularity? That pleasure needs to be
understood in more than just the traditionally appreciated 'enjoyments of the senses', like sex and food,
but that it inheres in the quality of the execution of
these activities and that, in turn, this reflects the skill
and timing of the participant. Without wanting to
suggest that something like this is necessary for pleasure to be experienced (in a Platonic sense?) we are
proposing that something like an ideal timing and,
thereby, a highly successful operation (in any field of
endeavour).

The problem is more complex. It is not merely a
matter of determining what and when would constitute a start to our pleasures; we face a comparable
dilemma in determining ends. At least literature and
myth provides us with an exemplary tale. I refer to
Krishna, the blue-god of Hinduism. When he made
love (and that seems to have been the major pre-occu-
pation of this god) he made it endlessly – a constant
pleasure to himself and his myriad 'cowherds' with
whom he made love simultaneously and without termination. Not as a super-stud, but as a lover who nev-

er came. Perfect timing without culmination. Krishna apparently never experienced ejaculation – not as a pathology demanding therapeutic attention but as a symbol of an ultimate bliss. And as such, thereby contradicting any alleged need for humans inexorably to expect pain at the end of pleasure. That is, not only does pleasure endure and not be short-lived – but, more significantly, there being no end. To be enjoyed purely: a pleasure without consequences, without further benefit or cost, without pain of the 'little death'. An allegory: reminding us, in part, of the impossibility of such a state of affairs. It may be wondrous to contemplate, but it is doomed to remain nothing more than mythology. Is the state of affairs depicted one of an absolute desire, no matter how impossible it may be to attain? Do the various representations of Krishna depict a sublimity, a perfect satisfaction? A totally unrestrained pursuit of sexual pleasures, without frustrations, failures and limitations? In a way this is so; but perhaps we need to complement , and thereby contradict, this imagery by suggesting that the Krishna myths also remind us of the insatiability of desire. That, irrespective of the heights of pleasure reached, we need to return and return to the same experience, to relive again a perfect joy – which inexplicably leaves us dissatisfied. We cannot live without pleasure. It is addictive; it is pain as well and we suffer accordingly.

What has been said may be perfectly reasonable for sexual pleasure but is it appropriate for other forms of pleasure: the delights of food for example. The joys of music – to listen or to perform – more doubtful, or is it that the duration of the pleasurable experience is just much longer than for that of sex, but that it has its own pleasure-span as well. Yet surely pleasure can come to us only now and then and only for limited periods of time. Pleasure does not drag on and on. It cannot in some constant manner hang over us. Even Krishna obviously sought it out. We may wallow in pain but not in pleasure. Pain and pleasure do not temporally balance each other. Only the former lingers and may become chronic – lasting a long time. Pleasure is the acute experience. (Acute – opposite of chronic – sharp, pointed, acting keenly on the senses, sensitive or responsive to impressions, finely-strung). An interesting opposition: one a quantity of time, a duration, a long duration; the other a quality of sensation. It is as if an intense sensation may be experienced only over a brief period of time.

Anything of lengthy duration must be experienced, it seems, as a dull, blunt, diluted sensation. Have we here a hierarchical comparison between the expected qualities of pain and pleasure – irrespective whether this is in any way an accurate portrayal? That is, pleasure is both intense and short-lived; pain is dull and abiding, lasting, durable, lifelong, tedious, interminable, persistent, constant, unchangeable, prolonged, protracted. A mixed quality both connoting either quite in-admirable qualities like tedious, or ambivalent ones like constant, unchangeable. Nothing certainly exciting or brilliant – or different. In contrast, Roget gives the following (a sample only) for Transience (the opposite of Long Duration): passing, fleeting, fugitive, precarious, volatile, fickle, capricious, throw-away, perishable, frail, fragile, provisional, doomed, short and sweet, quick, brisk, sudden, meteoric, like a flash, hasty, offhand, for the moment, for the time being. Rather unappealing?

In what direction and circularity are these associations going? Surely these words are more positively oriented, more attractive, more connected with pleasurable rather than uninteresting, unattractive, unappealing, unrewarding attributes and experiences.

A telling twist. These words, especially considered collectively, contain their own ambivalence – but a specific ambivalence – that is, pleasure is at the same time associated with pain. Do we culturally believe at some deep level that we cannot have the former without the latter as well (although we have pain without having pleasure somehow attached)? And if so, is it because of the inevitable pain of separation, of termination which must end all transient pleasure? It ends, all too soon. To the degree that this is so, is it because we have culturally, yet unconsciously, over associated pleasure with sexual pleasure, and the necessarily associated pain of 'the little death'. That fits the dual sensations. Other modes of pleasure do not – for example, the pleasure of music, of words, of the arts in general.

Have we unearthed the irony of pleasure? Ask Sudhir Kakar and John Ross, The ontogeny of love in their *Tales of Love, Sex and Danger* (1986).

The gift of timing.

Timing in the sense of perfect timing is a gift. A possession, a quality, a skill, a talent, to be envied. It is not something that can be easily learned or acquired by keen application. It would seem you have it or you do not have it. It comes naturally – or not at all. Having it makes you grateful for your good fortune. You do not surrender it; it is a gift that is not open to some form of circulation, or to be on some temporary loan, or to be pawned. Like a gift from the gods, you are or are not blessed with it, eternally. But we can conjecture further. Something so prized may have a price. We can, for example, become possessed by something highly valued. It may have a fascination we cannot resist. Timing can be used and misused; used for any end. A master thief and a master 'con' time their strikes deliberately, delicately, perfectly. It is not that they may act at any time; the moment has precision about it. The English word 'gift' originally came from the German 'gift', and in that language it means both marriage and poison. A gift has two faces. A talent can be utilised for good or for bad. But culturally the western world responds sympathetically to this talent irrespective of its use. We all display more than a sneaking respect for the thief and the con simply because of their 'artistry': the delicate cunning, the complexity and subtlety of its conception, the bravura of its execution, all excite us. Fiction, in novels or films, celebrate such feats of timing – as much as journalism denigrates the commonly alleged mistiming of police raids on suspected quarters – in which either innocents are raided by mistake or the culprits escape by even finer timing.

But timing, again perfect timing, is a gift in another special way. It is executed by, as it were, giving yourself, going with the flow. It is not a taking, a grabbing, a clawing. Yet it is a particular giving; not a surrender, a humiliation, certainly not a defeat. By this form of giving, and only by this form a giving, one gains. By giving in you do not diminish your own worth, nor enhance the worth of the other; rather, by giving yourself you further enable yourself. The power of others becomes your power. The giving has been, not a sign of weakness, but a sign of confidence and of strength. An opponent ought realistically fear such a gift. A situation of challenge no longer appears threatening let alone invincible once the sign of such a gift is glimpsed. The beginning of the end, an imminent victory sensed. You have won because you have dared to appear, at least to the foolish, weak. Perfect timing is that paradox: an apparent momentary surrender ensuring a success; a delicate power; a strength posed as a delicate thing. A deception. A feint.

Ever since Marcel Mauss wrote his classic essay on the gift, many scholars have added elaborations to the notion – all, in one way or other, confirming there is no such thing as a 'pure' gift. The gift of a perfectly timed action adds a further dimension to these studies. Here we have a gift which produces its own return-gift; it becomes instantaneously its own reward. One is not 'repaid', as if by others, as if in exchange for some gift. Nor is it a matter of a deferral of reward. In the act of giving you receive. The gift of timing casts doubt on the conventional (western?) dualities of exchange: in particular, those basic beliefs we automatically apply like the cost behind every benefit; the necessity for payment; the cliche that there is no such thing as a free lunch. All entertain ideas of some inexorable necessity of a price to be paid, of the operation of some cosmic law of interpersonal relations which imposes on humans a curse – you shall have to pay for whatever you receive; nothing is free. And is this not the premise from which all our (western) theories of economics ultimately derive? And, indirectly, our so-called common-sense about politics, that is, about pragmatic political behavior, which may possibly include all politics once we strip the deceptive veils of ideology and high morality from before our eyes. Timing as giving as a prelude to receiving challenges this tradition.

Timing, Chance – *and denial*

The more I consider timing, that is, the unexpected interruption, not the practitioner's delicate touch, the more it seems obvious that chance, in one form or another, determines so much of what we do. This is not because a God or a Fate propels us this way or that. It is essentially because we live in a complex world where everything interacts with the other. Man can never be an island. We cannot avoid whatever just happens, here or there; we have to adjust, every time, one way or another.

In a way, 'when' something happens is, perhaps, as important as the 'what' that happens, because the 'when' determines exactly what that 'what' will be. Chance is chancy. One never knows when a scandal, even a misuse of words, can emerge, explode, and change one's world. Yet western culture denies its role; we are too rational, scientific, for that, apparently. We are, we are told to believe, in control of ourselves.

But it is by chance that we are born. We rarely think that; it demeans our personal identity and worth. We deny it. But only one egg of all the eggs gets fertilised. You are the outcome of that arbitrary selection; you could have 'remained', for whatever that means, an unfertilised egg! It is also by chance that you are a female – or a male. As it is by chance that you are born an Australian, an Indian, a German, an Egyptian or a Chilean.

Likewise, the big things in global history are random. How many people expected Brexit? How many people predicted that America would be ruled by a dangerously unpredictable, psychologically disturbed proto-fascist at the beginning of 2017? Life in the western world has become even more unpredictable in this era of global terrorism. Think 9/11. It has generated something historically new; global guerrilla warfare, striking anywhere, anytime, anyhow, by anyone. Effective defense against it is impossible. Accordingly, western life, and death, have never been as arbitrary as now.

Timing, the impact of the unexpected on on-going affairs, bites the lives of us all, in arbitrary ways, as we go about our mundane activities; thereby destroying conventional notions of simple narrative, of ordered, constructed continuity of affairs, of linear development and change, of self-determination. Rather it highlights the mess of any life; how our oh-so human efforts to make the best of things are thwarted, time and again, and how we, so often, suddenly, have to react, readjust and change course. Things just happen, out of the blue, for good or bad – the power of chance, the unexpected, luck, the arbitrary.

That is the essence of the ancient belief in, and

formulation of Fate: that we delude ourselves if we believe we are in control, that, with confidence, we plan and determine our future. I wonder, at times, whether creating the word and imagery of 'Fate' was a clever, indeed sophisticated way of psychologically immunising us to the bitter reality of the limitation of humans to shape their own destiny.

Management in large modern, efficient organisations is a paradigm of western modernity. Studies show that planned work for the office day gets interrupted on average every eleven minutes, taking another eleven minutes, on average, to return to the intended tasks. Half of each day is occupied by chance distraction. Nothing suggests that we must not plan; but it says clearly 'do not foolishly assume that your plan will automatically bear fruit'.

It is not strange that nothing of significance throughout the twentieth century was foreseen. And that includes the actual outbreak of the two world wars; that varying efforts to avoid war were proceeding to the very end shows nothing was inevitable, and that no-one was certain of either a good or bad outcome. What happened, every now and then, was a surprise to some degree or other. Even which nations were likely to be allies was uncertain. There, as elsewhere, human action is invariably a reaction to a reaction. In a way, 'best of luck' seems a timely wish, always.

We humans seem highly tuned to the need of a certain simplicity of affairs, past and present, and a reliability of prediction. Derrida warns us of un-cluttered readings of the past and of the assumed, obvious errors of leaders and influential writers at the time. When we look back, everything seems so simple and determined; never a hint that things can happen idiosyncratically. Each occasion is a once-off phenomenon. Life is not a piece of theatre, in which we have learned our lines. No moment of life can be rehearsed. As Freud emphasised:

> If one considers chance to be unworthy of deter-mining our fate, it is simply a relapse into the pious view of the universe which Leonardo was on the way to overcoming when he wrote that the sun does not move. We naturally feel hurt that a just God and a kindly providence do not protect us better ... At the same time we are all too ready to forget that in fact everything we do in our life is chance. (Freud, 1910).

By chance, as I write this, I notice the publication of a book by Robert Frank, *Success and Luck*, explaining how luck is playing an increasing role in world affairs. I wonder, however, whether luck's role is actually in-creasing; rather, that the West has taken a long time indeed to admit luck's pervasive presence. Rather, de-spite that reality, we embrace the popular myth: the repetition that rational beings essentially succeed in planning and implementing their progress. As the an-cient Mexican saying goes; 'If you want to make God laugh, tell Him your plans'.

When we look at the future, two operations are 'naturally' involved. With varying degrees of effort and skill we try to anticipate the many factors involved and, accordingly, make provisional decisions about the odds; and we feel shades of optimism or pessimism. And we hope. We hope we will be successful; we hope it will work; we hope nothing gets in the way; we hope, despite all signs, that things may finally turn out for the good. Hope surely is a universal human quality – along with notions of trust, goodwill, caution, doubt, fear, hate, love. Hope exists to compensate the unpleasant actuality that the future is open-ended. If the future were certain, there would be no need for it. So, hope illustrates two inherent aspects of human existence: that we can never positively know the future, for if that were not so, hope would be a totally irrelevant human attribute. We automatically have hope, because of the lack of assurance. Hope also exists because of the possibility of a good outcome, hope is always, also a wish for a successful result. Language is very much a human matter; not an accidental affair. Doubt, possibility, hope are all basic aspects of being human in an unpredictable world.

At this horrible, destructive moment of history many wretched human beings have lost the element of hope; to them, time will never again change; there is no future; life will end, just as it is. To lose the faculty of hope must be one of the greatest human tragedies; no sense of anticipation, of possibility, of a future.

Time and life appear ended – their only certainty.

Hope quietly displays this chanciness of human existence. Yet few people pay attention to Nietzsche's (wistful?) hope that the brave historian of the future – taking note of this unpredictability – will always say 'perhaps'. Unfortunately, in its place, certainty, clarity, simplicity rule. Will the West ever accept the fact that modern western men and women, and their society are nothing like what the Enlightenment preaches: rational beings, rid of superstition, successfully planning and implementing their progress? An internalised idea of 'perhaps' could, perhaps, better prepare us to face life's whims.

The means of obtaining a future well-being is an endless riddle. A planned and successful life is, in a way, a tragic myth. Truly 'mission impossible'. Can we learn to accept the dominant role of chance in our lives – without being overwhelmed by the realisation? We acknowledge the reality of inevitable death, normally without traumatic consequences. Just as we know, and accept, that we cannot fly. In a way chance is determined; an inevitable product of the messiness of human life. Can we face the fact that chance is just another given?

Perhaps we could take comfort from Agathon, the little known Greek tragic poet and playwright of the fifth century BCE, when he wrote 'art loves chance and chance loves art'. We don't know if and how he elaborated that. But how fascinating that such a profound, yet intriguing observation – which could easily be taken as the apercu of some post-modernist French thinker - was in fact gleaned two and a half millennia ago. And we talk about 'progress' as a unique feature of modern humanity!

Enlightenment ideology broadcasts that we are all running along the same path planning our future of progress, upon a level-playing temporal space called time. But, instead of some constant forward travel we, surely, at times go backwards, or sideways, in a milliard of orientations. Even that is inadequate. Time has been naturally assumed by the West to have direction, an orientation. It is always depicted graphically in terms of a line. Understandable perhaps; but, if not misleading, then at least it locks us into one scenario, and taken as a truth. Can we forget that imagery and provide a new one for ourselves?

Perhaps we are just running around in circles, irregular ones. Or, to adopt the language of certain non-western cultures and think of life more as 'playing', seriously, an endless game. Or, more dramatically, performing a theatrical play interminably. The West obsessively clings to the idea that everything has an inherent potential for measurement and assessment. It appears unable to face the possibility that life, and time, are perhaps beyond precise calibration. Perhaps we can learn, alternatively, to appreciate more the richness and the mystery of life and time. And maybe think of new myths, linking the elements of challenge, passion, fallibility. Why can we not say 'Life, as well as art, loves chance, change and endless mystery'.

Is it possible that we have failed so dramatically to understand ourselves because we have been fooled by language: hence failing to see that life and time and chance are all one: each, in a way, being a euphemism, and hence, a mirror of the others. Let us aim even more radically; time needs to be seen as a quality as much if not more, as a motion.

But chance does not exist, independently, in a vacuum. Freud may have over-simplified the situation. Life operates in a complex union of rhythmic time beats. There is, in the background a continuo (unceasing continuity, perpetuity, harmony, cadence, monotone, score) of what could be called 'administration' or 'management': a constant, daily and interminable repetition of a task – government bureaucracy being an ideal model; the regular preparation of meals another. It is inevitably present; and it will continue till the end of time. No change involved, except in minutiae.

At another level of activity, certain roles continue to be performed with the appropriate, local repetitions: a doctor, a teacher, a mechanic, a journalist, the list is long, continue to operate, each with its recognisable, though variable beat. Playing to that backdrop is the periodic repetition of the anniversary. No surprise is involved; big and small, public and private re-visitations of past events form a permanent part of the annual calendar. They constitute time-out episodes from routine behavior, administration.

A radically different time score is involved in what could be called 'movements': those changes that emerge and slowly stretch over time in their particular forms of significance. Global warming a notable identity. Liberation and the legitimacy of sexual and gender differentiations being, in the western world in particular, another more recent movement.

Industrialisation, developing over the last three hundred years in the western world, and now following suit elsewhere, brings a new and greater consistency of human activity. As has digitally-produced change.

And the permanence of bipolarised differences and cultural identity: urban versus rural; rich versus poor; educated versus uneducated; young versus the old; the healthy versus the sickly. All, in a way, centered around the clash between tradition and novelty; old ways against the new. Some movements overlap with others – some clash, others cohere. A certain predictability and uniformity operate, as distinct, unbridgeable divisions consolidate. All these features collectively reduce surprise and chance to some degree, as they compartmentalise calls to improvise, to handle a new situation.

It is against this backdrop of continuities that periodic, unexpected chance, small and large events erupt and demand attention; at both personal and global levels of life. Within this remarkably complex, cross-cutting human scenario, 'things just happen' which can momentarily distract or even radically disrupt and change life's daily manner. Do we know what we will be doing in one year's time? Yes and no. Are we making 'progress'? A meaningless question. Are we heading in some determinate direction? Hardly. Is our life one of rational calculation leading to some planned personal or collective behavior? Certainly not.

With these continuing manifold operations, the thunder of certain momentous chance events – a natural disaster, a clash of cultures, nations, may cause mass disturbance, radical re-alignments, re-focusing of attention, deep concern, intervention, and local and global conflict can appear – with no one reliable outcome predictable. The world can change overnight. The world can quickly become even a giddier mess; a begetter of tragedy, such as the current, spectacle of mass displaced peoples. Are we models of Enlightenment when we think of the sixty-five million displaced humans around the globe?

About the same time that Freud pronounced the human inevitability of chance, Nietzsche, that man so alert to human foibles, wrote 'No conqueror believes in chance'. The word does not exist in the vocabulary of the 'successful'. They can never concede their good luck.

We, the collective proud bearers of the western Enlightenment exemplify Nietzsche's prediction: we believe the last three hundred years of the West has been an unqualified success. And 'we' got there, we say, because of our reason and science, as well as our superior moral, Christian code of behavior. Chance with its favourable or unfavourable timing has no place in our consciousness. We live a life of denial. This blind arrogance is not a sole specialty of our warrior and political and business leaders; it is as well, perhaps unwittingly, our educational leaders. Chance, along with 'other' superstitious beliefs and practices, are anathema; never to appear in scholarly curricula.

What of an education that excludes compassion, passion, emotion, excitement, sexuality, disorder, confusion, mess, contradictions, ambiguity, uncertainty, doubt, time, unpredictability, the hybrid, the complex, art, chance, the poetic, the rhetorical, metaphoric, imaginative, speculative, heretical, mystery, puzzlement, the unseemly, the odious – and perhaps, all problematics?

The Enlightenment message is a powerful one. With rational thought and science allegedly at our disposal, we believe we are both free and master of ourselves. In time we will be master of nature and of the universe – at least we used to say that. We are given no other story. No wonder the West proudly suffers hubris.

Our self-image leans towards the kitsch. Our faults dismissed as the occasional aberration from the norm; the exception which clearly proves the rule. How does one go about educating the West to think more deeply about the mysteries and richness of time and, in particular, how does one lead people to appreciate how timing, how chance, determines so much of what we do and don't do in our lives? How does one successfully eradicate mass denial?

Can I expect people to forego the comforting self-satisfaction of believing, in good and simple faith, that their reasoning powers have abundantly and reliably benefited man, and will conquer the world, while all I have to offer as an alternative is the promise of the relative unpredictability of reality, and the likely inadequacy, expedience, short-sightedness, and opportunism of our thoughts and actions to respond effectively to the unexpected, the timely and the untimely, which will certainly visit us again and again, simply with what we 'have on hand', and perhaps more importantly, significantly, what we 'have on mind'?

What are my chances?

Only time can tell.

Permissions

We thank the original editors and journals for the re-publication of these chapters as follows:

'Political Time', which first appeared as 'Political Time: the Problem of time and chance', in *Time and Society* 2:2 (1993).

'To Play with Time' was 'To seduce or to flirt, that is the question', in *Time and Society* 12:2/3 (2003).

'Anticipating Future time' was 'Anticipation', in the *Australian Book Review* 198 (Feb/Mar 1998).

'Quality Time', appeared in *TIME, Perspectives at the Millennium* (The Study of Time X). Edited by M. P. Soulsby and J.T. Fraser. Bergin & Garvey: Westport, CT (2001).

Bibliography

As-Saffar, M. (1992). *Disorienting Encounters*. Trans. Susan George Miller. Berkeley: California University Press.

Barthes, R. (1982). *Camera Lucida*. London: Cape.

Borges, J.L. (1964). *Labyrinths*. Harmondsworth: Penguin.

Brooks, P. (1977). 'Freuds Masterplot'. *Yale French Studies* 55/57: 280-300.

Cirlot J.E. (1962). *A Dictionary of Symbols*. New York: Dutton.

Cixous, H. (1991). *Readings: The Poetics of Blanchot, Joyce, Kafka, Kleist, Lispector, and Tvetayeva*. Minneapolis: University of Minnesota Press.

Debord, G. (1994 [1967]). *The Society of the Spectacle.* New York: Zone Books.

Derrida, J. (1978) *Writing and Difference*. Trans. Alan Bass. Chicago: The University of Chicago Press.

Derrida, J. (1992) *The Other Heading: Reflections on Today's Europe*. Bloomington: Indiana University Press.

Derrida J. (1994). 'The Deconstruction of Actuality.' *Radical Philosophy* 68: 28-40.

Derrida J. (1995). *Archive Fever: A Freudian Impression..* Chicago: University of Chicago Press.

Derrida, J. (2003). *The Work of Mourning*. Chicago: University of Chicago Press.

Douez, S. (2001). 'Genome Hysteria', *The Age*. 15 May.

Ellingsen, P. (2001). 'A Breed Apart', *The Age*. 29 May.

Feyerabend, P. (2000). 'Letter to the Reader', recently discovered manuscript, *London Review of Books*. 22 June.

Foucault, M. (1973 [1963]). *The Birth of the Clinic: An Archeology of Medical Perception*. Trans. Alan Sheridan, London: Tavistock.

Foucault, M. (1990 [1984]). *The Use of Pleasure*. London: Vintage.

Frayn, M. (1998). *Copenhagen*. London: Methuen.

Freud, S. (1957 [1910]) 'Leonardo da Vinci and a memory of his Childhood'. In *The Standard Edition of the Complete Psychological Works of Sigmund Freud*, Volume 11. Edited by J. Strachey. London: Hogarth Press.

Freud, S. (1959 [1916]). 'On Transcience'. In *The Standard Edition of the Complete Psychological Works of Sigmund Freud*, Volume 14. Edited by J. Strachey. London: Hogarth Press.

Freud, S. (1922). 'Beyond the Pleasure Principle'. *Sigmund Freud*. Volume 4, London: International Psycho-analytical Press.

Freud, S. (1971 [1925]). 'A Note Upon the "Mystic Writing Pad"'. In *The Standard Edition of the Complete Psychological*

Works of Sigmund Freud, Volume 21 (1923-1925). Edited by J. Strachey. London: Hogarth Press.

Gadamer, H. (1988). 'The Drama of Zarathustra'. In *Nietzsche's New Seas*. Edited by M.A. Gillespie and T. B. Strong. Chicago: University of Chicago Press. 220-231.

Gadamer, H. (2003). *The Beginning of Knowledge*. Trans. Rod Coltman, New York: Continuum.

Griffiths, J. (2000). *Pip Pip: A Sideways Look at Time*. London: Flamingo.

Gudrin, R. (1997). *Time and The Art of Living*. Boston: Marliner Books.

Kakar, S and Ross, J. (1986). *Tales of Love, Sex and Danger*. Delhi: Oxford University Press.

Kermode, F. (2001). 'Maximum Assistance', *London Review of Books*. 22 February.

Kundera, M. (1996). *Testaments Betrayed: An Essay in Nine Parts*. New York: Harper Perennial.

Lacoue-Labarthe, P. (1900). *Heidegger, Art and Politics*. Oxford: Basil Blackwell.

Levi-Strauss, C. (1966 [1962]). *The Savage Mind*. London: Weidenfeld and Nicolson.

McCourt F. (1996). *Angela's Ashes*. London: HarperCollins.

Nehamas, A. (2000). 'Not Rocket Science', *London Review of Books*. 22 June.

Nietzsche F. (1989). *Ecce Homo (and On the Genealogy of Morals)*. Trans. W. Kaufmann. New York: Vintage Books.

Nkosi, L. (2000). 'An UnAmerican in New York', *London Review of Books*. 24 August.

Perec, G. (1989). *W, or The Memory of Childhood*. London: Collins Harvill.

Phillips, A. (1994). *On Flirtation*. London: Faber & Faber.

Phillips, A. (1996). *Monogamy*. New York: Pantheon Books.

Phillips, A. (2000). 'Unfathomable Craziness', *London Review of Books*. 18 May.

Rushdie S. (1981). *Midnight's Children*. London: Jonathan Cape.

Vitiello, V. (1996). 'Towards a Topology of the Religious'. In *Religion*. Edited by J. Derrida and G. Vattimo. Stanford: Stanford University Press. 136-69.

Wolpert, L. (2001). 'Desperately Seeking Certainty', *The Age*. 24 March.

Lightning Source UK Ltd.
Milton Keynes UK
UKHW040634230621
386017UK00002B/179

9 781838 013707